D1554835

How To
Qualify For The
Celestial
Kingdom
Today

By James B. Cox

NATIONAL MARKETING, INC.

Second Edition
First printing, November 1984 (2M)
Second printing, July 1986 (2M)
Third printing, August 1988 (2M)
Fourth printing, February 1990 (2.5M)
Fifth printing, September 1991 (2.5M)
Sixth printing, September 1992 (2.5M)
Seventh printing, May 1995 (2.5M)
Eighth printing, January 1998 (2.5M)
Ninth printing, November 2001 (3.0M)
ISBN 0-9646887-0-0

SKU #1100027

Published by
National Marketing, Inc.
P.O. Box 728
Santa Clara, UT 84765-0728

Cover design by James Fedor

PRINTED IN THE UNITED STATES OF AMERICA

Table of Contents

Dedicated to . . .

Those who have helped me to apply the gospel
correctly in my life:
*Mary Anna, Jeaneice, Deborah, Teresa,
Julianne, David, Eric, and Curtis.*

INTRODUCTION

Are you qualified for the celestial kingdom? Do you feel that if the Savior came today and the resurrection were to take place now, you would receive a celestial body? Can you say in your heart, "I am ready to meet the Savior"?

How do you feel about yourself? Are you excited about who you are, what you are doing, and what your potential is? Do you know that the course you are on is acceptable to Heavenly Father and his Son? Do you feel it is possible for one to sin and still feel good about himself?

How does God feel about you? Does he love you even when you sin? Does he walk with you daily? Can you feel his influence giving you direction every day? Do you know how to receive this direction daily? Do you know how to prepare for revelation, and can you tell when it comes? How can you know that your daily progress is acceptable to Heavenly Father, that he is pleased?

Do you know how to overcome the effects of sin? That is, do you know how to do away with the emotional drain that comes from past sins? Are you able to recall past mistakes and not feel emotionally bad but emotionally good about your life?

Have you learned how to overcome doubt? Have you learned how to create good feelings about yourself? Do you understand the importance of not judging yourself? Do you ever feel uncomfortable when you attend Church meetings and you are not doing *all* the speakers talk about?

Do you feel peace and joy in your heart at all times? Do you feel it is possible to have peace and joy at all times?

Do you feel that this life is a burden, with too much to do and not enough time? Do you feel like a failure with your children, your work, your physical fitness, or your Church work? Do you wonder if you will ever make it in this life?

It is the purpose of this book to discuss in detail what it takes to qualify for the celestial kingdom today. It will also talk about how Heavenly Father feels about each of us, how we can feel his love in our daily lives, how to stay in the strait and narrow path each day, and how to walk with the companionship of the Holy Ghost.

The following materials were taken from various authors, prophets, and from the scriptures. I have experienced these principles and concepts over the last twenty years so I know they are true. Hopefully, I have acknowledged all authors as various ideas are discussed. I would like to pay special tribute to Dr. Sterling Ellsworth, from whom I learned the truth about performance and the feelings of self-worth, and to Dr. Jonathan M. Chamberlain for his work on self-defeating behavior. Especially, I appreciate the long hours of review and the many suggestions given by Dr. Burton C. Kelly and Dr. Richard Ellsworth.

A Few Basic Principles

Before we can truly begin to progress, we must make certain our actions are based on true principles. Here are five principles that are so fundamental we should keep them in mind throughout the entire book:

Principle No. 1
What we believe to be true determines our actions

Suppose a man is climbing to the top of a mountain. As he approaches the top, he meets a six-foot grizzly bear. He needs to make a decision quickly. Should he run down the hill, hoping to outrun the bear, or go up to the bear, shake hands with him, and ask him the golden questions? At last he decides to shake hands. Why? Because he has heard that a film company is making a movie on bears at the top of this mountain on this very day. He chooses to believe that this bear is really a man dressed in a bear skin.

This man's actions are based upon what he believes to be true and not necessarily upon what *is* true. This principle of action based on belief works in every aspect of our lives.

What would happen if you chose to believe everyone liked you (even if some didn't)? If you really believed this, how would you treat them? You would be kind, and sweet, open with them; you would show them respect. If some showed disrespect to you or would not talk to you, you would assume they had had a bad day or that perhaps someone had treated them badly.

If you continued this course, eventually you would find that even those who did not like you at first would come to have respect for you. Why? Because people cannot continue to dislike a person who always treats them kindly, who points out their good qualities when talking of them with others. This is the attitude God has asked us to develop. (2 Nephi 31:20.) "For we must love God and all men."

But what would happen if you chose to dislike some people (perhaps because you felt they did not like you)? You would begin to treat them disrespectfully. Though they were nice to you, you would not trust them; you would wonder what they were up to. As a result, though they did like you at first, they would eventually come to feel uncomfortable with you and dislike many things about you.

Principle No. 2

Results are based on what is true

Apply Principle No. 1 to the following situation: A man jumps off a two-story building believing that he will not be hurt. His action is based upon what he believes to be true. However, when he hits the ground, he breaks his back and one leg and cracks several ribs. The results of his jump are inevitably based upon what *is* true when one jumps off a building, regardless of what he believes to be true.

If one chooses to believe that stealing is okay because everyone does it, he has not looked at the inevitable results of such a decision. When he is caught, what he believes to be true will have no effect on the demands of justice. In fact, even if he is never caught, justice will receive its just due in other effects in this life and in the next.

Principle No. 3

Most things we believe are learned

For example, how should one keep the Sabbath day holy? Indeed, which day of the week is "the" day to rest from our labors? What should we do to keep this day holy? What are the benefits of keeping it holy? Answers to these questions are learned through experience. We are not born with these answers.

This is true for all of life's deep questions — the need for honesty, chastity, modesty, the need to love and be loved, the need for education, the need to raise a family, the need to be a good marriage partner. Associated questions, such as how to set goals, how to plan, how to organize one's time, how to cope with today's economic pressures, how to earn a living or build an estate, or how to do missionary work or genealogy work, are all answered through experience, through the things we learn. Problems arise when we have learned and accepted truths; untruths about ourselves, or about others, or about God, or how we will gain salvation.

As we study together be prepared to evaluate your beliefs. In finding truth, Principle No. 4 is the key for knowing truth so that one is not "tossed to and fro and carried about with every wind of doctrine." (Ephesians 4:14.)

Principle No. 4

"And by the power of the Holy Ghost ye may know the truth of all things." (Moroni 10:5.)

Learn to listen to the Holy Spirit. "I will tell you in your mind and in your heart, by the Holy Ghost.... " (D&C 8:2.) Listen to your mind and heart. The Holy Ghost will help you as you progress toward the celestial kingdom. The Savior said that the Holy Ghost "shall teach you all things, and bring all things to your remembrance, whatsoever I have said unto you." (John 14:26.) He will guide you in all truth and will only say what the Father and the Son would say. (John 16:13.) He will "show unto you all things what ye should do." (2 Nephi 32:5.) Let this special gift of guidance by the Holy Spirit give you direction and understanding. Listen through your heart *and* mind, and not by your mind alone.

Principle No. 4 teaches us an important truth about self-worth:

Do not believe something about yourself unless you have received a confirmation from the Holy Ghost. For example, one sister came to me with a problem. Her husband was going to leave her. They had exchanged harsh words and had thrown a few things at each other. She said, "I guess I am not a good wife or mother. I have driven my husband from the home. It is my fault and even God does not like me anymore. I might as well quit."

I said, "You mean when you prayed this morning, you got

down on your knees and said, 'Heavenly Father, I guess I am no good, you do not like me anymore. I have failed as a wife and mother, so what is the use of continuing?' And the Lord answered back, 'That is correct, my daughter; I do not like you anymore. I knew you would never make it. I am glad you have finally realized it.'"

Now of course, God did not say any such thing! She had not checked with him about these conclusions. These conclusions were from Satan, not from God. She had not prayed about them. She had allowed Satan to whisper to her, and she had accepted his whisperings.

Principle No. 5
Each individual is responsible for his own growth

The law of free agency precludes anyone's taking over your responsibility for your salvation. Only you can choose and act for yourself. Others can persuade, motivate, and inspire you, but only you can give yourself direction and purpose by these influences.

Samuel the Lamanite said:

> *And now remember, remember, my brethren, that whosoever perisheth, perisheth unto himself; and whosoever doeth iniquity, doeth it unto himself; for behold, ye are free; ye are permitted to act for yourself; for behold, God hath given unto you a knowledge and he hath made you free. (Helaman 14:30.)*

Life is like piloting an airplane. Others can teach you, be examples for you, inspire and support you, but you still must learn to fly the plane alone. You must choose where your plane will fly, when and how long it will fly, and where it will land. Someone else may tell you what to do and where to go, but you must choose to obey, and you still must fly alone. You are responsible. You build and experience your belief system. The power to modify your life lies within your reach and no one else's. Upon request Heavenly Father is always available to help you, but even then you are still responsible for your choices.

Section I

A PERFECT BRIGHTNESS OF HOPE

So you want to qualify for the celestial kingdom today. Do you have a "perfect brightness of hope"? That is, if the Savior came today, is there no question in your mind that you are prepared? Can you imagine within yourself the Savior saying to you "Come unto me ye blessed, for behold, your works have been the works of righteousness upon the face of the earth"? (Alma 5:16.)

Or are you filled with doubt and discouragement? Do you feel that there is too much to do, that you will never make it anyway, so why keep trying? Your flame of hope is almost out, and you often feel the Church is a burden rather than a blessing. You know the Church is true; you love the prophets, and are excited about all the good the Church is accomplishing, but you feel unworthy to even picture yourself gaining a celestial body.

Hope is so important that we must have it before we can progress farther. The purpose of this section is to help each of us gain that perfect brightness of hope, so we will gain that great gift of eternal life and experience peace and joy from this knowledge and confirmation.

The following chapters develop the perceptions it will take for each of us to qualify for the celestial kingdom today. At the end of this section suggested assignments are given so that one can make these perceptions of the gospel his own and feel the joy and peace that come from correct application of these principles.

The first chapter will review the plan of salvation and help answer two big questions: (1) How long do I have to qualify for the celestial kingdom, and (2) how long do I have to qualify for eternal life?

The second chapter will cover what the scriptures and the prophets say must be done to qualify for the celestial kingdom today. The third chapter will ask questions about man's journey to gain eternal life and give some answers. Pray before you read these chapters—open your mind to revelation, understanding, and especially to the confirmation of the Holy Ghost. Unless a person is basically unrepentant, he should come to the end of this material with a new feeling of hope.

Chapter One

Plan of Salvation and The Celestial Kingdom

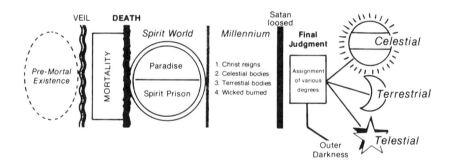

WE HAVE BEEN TAUGHT by the prophets, and it has been confirmed by the Holy Ghost, that the plan of salvation outlined above is true. That is, each of us existed before we came to earth. (D&C 93:29.) Heavenly Father is the Father of our spirits. (Romans 8:26.) We lived in premortal life as spirit children of Heavenly Parents (Abraham 3:22-25, Jeremiah 1:4-5), and when we agreed on the plan of salvation we shouted for joy. (Job 38:4-7.) A veil was placed over our minds so we could not recall our premortal life with Heavenly Father.

We have been placed in mortality for several reasons. First, to gain a body like our Heavenly Parents, and second, to qualify for a kingdom of glory. (D&C 130:22; Abraham 3:26-26, D&C 88:27-32.)

Most of us will experience physical death in this life. Others, who are righteous on the earth when the Savior comes, will not taste of death, but will live to old age and then be changed in a twinkling of an eye. (D&C 63:50-51.) The righteous who die before the Millennium will be received into a state of happiness called paradise.

> *And then shall it come to pass, that the spirits of those who are righteous are received into a state of happiness, which is called paradise, a state of rest, a state of peace, where they shall rest from all their troubles and from all their cares, and sorrows.* (Alma 40:12.)

Another blessing for those who qualify for paradise is that they will no longer be tempted by Satan. [1]

Joseph Fielding Smith defined the righteous as "those who have been baptized and who have been faithful." These, he taught, "are gathered in one part and all the others in another part of the spirit world." [2] Those who die before the age of eight are among the righteous.

Can one qualify for paradise after death?

It appears that spirits in prison can repent and then dwell with the righteous in paradise.

> Repentance opens the prison doors to the spirits in hell; it enables those bound with the chains of hell to free themselves from darkness, unbelief, ignorance, and sin. As rapidly as they can overcome these obstacles—gain light, believe truth, acquire intelligence, cast off sin, and

---

1. Bruce R. McConkie, *Mormon Doctrine*, 2nd ed. (Bookcraft, 1966,) p. 782.
2. Joseph Fielding Smith, *Doctrines of Salvation*, (Bookcraft 1967,) 2:230.

break the chains of hell—they can leave the hell that imprisons them and dwell with the righteous in the peace of paradise. [3]

Millennium Begins

When Jesus Christ returns to earth, several events will take place that have great interest for each of us. The Millennium will begin wherein Christ will preside over the earth for one thousand years. (D&C 29:11.) The righteous who are in the grave as well as those who are on the earth will be lifted up to meet the Savior when he comes. (D&C 88:96-97.) Then the earth, as well as the wicked who are upon the earth, will be burned. The wicked will go to spirit prison and the earth will become paradisiacal, fit for terrestrial habitation. Satan will be bound so he will not have a place in the hearts of man. (D&C 45:55.)

Morning of the First Resurrection — Celestial Bodies

Those individuals who are lifted up to meet the Savior when he comes are qualified to receive celestial bodies. Those in the grave will receive theirs the moment they are lifted up. Those who are alive upon the earth when the Savior comes will be quickened with a "millennial-type" body and will receive their celestial body in a twinkling of an eye when they reach the age of one hundred. [4]

"Afternoon" of the First Resurrection — Terrestrial Bodies

And after this another angel shall sound, which is the second trump; and then cometh the redemption of those who are Christ's at his coming; who have received their part in that prison which is prepared for them, that they might receive the Gospel, and be judged according to men in the flesh. (D&C 88:99.)

---

3. Bruce R. McConkie, *Mormon Doctrine*, p. 755.

4. Bruce R. McConkie, *The Millennial Messiah*, (Deseret Book, 1982,) p. 648.

This is the afternoon of the first resurrection; it takes place after our Lord has ushered in the millennium. Those coming forth at that time do so with terrestrial bodies. [5]

These are they who rejected the gospel on the earth but afterward accepted it in spirit prison. They were blinded by the craftiness of men on earth but were honorable. (D&C 76:73-78.) These also are they who accepted the gospel upon the earth but were not valiant in their testimony of Jesus Christ while upon the earth. (D&C 76:79.)

Joseph Fielding Smith reviews the resurrection of terrestrial bodies as follows:

> In this resurrection will come forth those of the terrestrial order, who were not worthy to be caught up to meet him, but who are worthy to come forth to enjoy the millennial reign.... Also in this class will be numbered those who died without law and hence are not under condemnation for a violation of the commandments of the Lord. The promise is made to them of redemption from death in the following words: *and then shall the heathen nations be redeemed, and they that knew no law shall have part in the first resurrection; and it shall be tolerable for them.* (D&C 45:54.) These, too, shall partake of the mercies of the Lord and shall receive the reuniting spirit and body inseparably, thus becoming immortal, but not with the fulness of the glory of God. [6]

Judgments

We can see that several judgments take place throughout the plan of salvation. Before birth, each was judged in determining where and when on earth he would live. Those who die before the Millennium occurs will be judged in order to determine if they

---

5. Bruce R. McConkie, *Mormon Doctrine*, p. 640.

6. Joseph Fielding Smith, *Doctrines of Salvation*, 2:296-97.

go to paradise or spirit prison. When the Savior comes it must be determined who qualifies to be lifted up to meet him and hence qualifies for a celestial body. When the earth is cleansed by fire the wicked will also be removed from the earth life and sent to spirit prison and therefore another judgment takes place. And finally, who qualifies for a terrestrial body will be determined in the afternoon of the first resurrection.

Final Judgment

What is left to judge at the final judgment? The scriptures tell us that before this event can occur, Satan will be loosed for a season to gather his armies. (D&C 88:111.) Those in spirit prison shall be resurrected with either a telestial body or with an unglorified body to be cast out into outer darkness. This is called the second or last resurrection. (D&C 88:24, 31-32.)

At the final judgment our inheritances are given to us by our Heavenly Father. It is over. Our days of preparation are finished. It is time for us to sit at the table and enjoy the feast. This is the time when worthy people will be assigned to one of the three levels of glory in the celestial kingdom. There are also levels in the lesser kingdoms. In the telestial kingdom there are different degrees, "as one star differs from another star in glory, even so differs one from another in glory in the telestial world." (D&C 76:98.) Those persons who will be cast into outer darkness will be so assigned.

This is the day when we shall pause and review our mortal life upon the earth, our premortal and post-mortal life, and reflect with awe. We will be pleased that we fulfilled the law, kept the commandments, overcame the world, suffered but endured, sacrificed, found forgiveness, walked by faith and found strength in it, and, most of all, experienced the love that Heavenly Father had for us throughout these various stages of life. We will be able to look into the faces of our Heavenly Parents and with tears in our eyes thank them for their helping us to qualify for the great gift of eternal life. It is finished, and we have arrived.

Question: How long does one have in which to qualify for a celestial body?

Answer: In Alma 34:32 we read:

> For behold, this life is the time for men to prepare to meet God; yea, behold **the day** of this life is the day for men to perform their labors.

Amulek in Alma 34:35 warns:

> For behold, if ye have procrastinated the day of repentance even until death, behold, ye have become subjected to the spirit of the devil, and he doth seal you his; therefore, the Spirit of the Lord hath withdrawn from you, and hath no place in you, and the devil hath all power over you; and this is the final state of the wicked.

Apostle Melvin J. Ballard gives us greater insight into Amulek's words:

> But this life is the time in which men are to repent. Do not let any of us imagine that we can go down to the grave not having overcome the corruptions of the flesh and then lose in the grave all our sins and evil tendencies. They will be with us. They will be with the spirit when separated from the body.
>
> It is my judgment that any man or woman can do more to conform to the laws of God in one year in this life than they could in ten years when they are dead. The spirit only can repent and change, and then the battle has to go forward with the flesh afterwards. It is much easier to overcome and serve the Lord when both flesh and spirit are combined as one. This is the time when men are more pliable and susceptible. We will find when we are dead every desire, every feeling will be greatly intensified. When clay is pliable it is much easier to change than when it gets hard and sets.
>
> This life is the time to repent. That is why I presume it will take a thousand years after the first resurrection until the last group will be prepared to come forth. It will take them a thousand years to do what it would have

taken, but threescore years and ten to accomplish in this life.[7]

President Joseph F. Smith suggests that the best time to overcome the weaknesses of the flesh is now:

> ...When we go out of this life, leave this body, we will desire to do many things that we cannot do at all without the body. We will be seriously handicapped, and we will long for the body; we will pray for that early reunion with our bodies. We will know then what advantage it is to have a body.
>
> Then, every man and woman who is putting off until the next life the task of correcting and overcoming the weakness of the flesh are sentencing themselves to years of bondage, for no man or woman will come forth in the resurrection until they have completed their work, until they have overcome, until they have done as much as they can do.[8]

Now, consider when will we be eligible for the inheritance of a celestial body? For those who are in the spirit world, it is when the Savior returns to earth and the Millennium begins. For those who are living on the earth, when the Savior comes, it will be when they reach the age of man, or old age, and shall be changed in a twinkling of an eye. (D&C 63:50-51.)

Bruce R. McConkie reviews the morning of the first resurrection:

> Those being resurrected with celestial bodies, whose destiny is to inherit a celestial kingdom, will come forth in the morning of the first resurrection. Their graves shall be opened and they shall be caught up to meet the Lord at his Second Coming.[9]

7. Melvin J. Ballard, *Three Degrees of Glory*, pamphlet, second renewal, Salt Lake City, Utah; (Magazine Printing and Publishing, 1975,) p. 12.

8. Spencer W. Kimball, *The Miracle of Forgiveness*, (Bookcraft, 1969,) p. 11.

9. Bruce R. McConkie, *Mormon Doctrine*, p. 640.

It appears that the best time to repent and become clean is today. Why? We do not know how long we have on the earth. Today may be our last day; therefore, today is not only our best day to repent, it may be our only day.

Question: How long does one have to qualify for exaltation?

Answer: As far as becoming perfect to gain the highest degree of the celestial kingdom, we have this life of mortality, plus the spirit world time, assuming we die before the Second Coming, plus 1,000 years of the Millennium. The final judgment does not take place until the end of the Millennium. The key is *to qualify* for a celestial inheritance each day and not be so concerned about perfection *now*. By so doing, we will receive a celestial body when the Savior comes and then we can continue to progress until we are able to develop the attributes of God. Thus, we become perfect even as our Father in Heaven is perfect.

During the Millennium, Satan will be tied up for 1,000 years and Jesus Christ will preside over his people. (D&C 88:110.) All the telestial filth will be burned from the earth; that is, all the R and X movies, drugs, pornography, etc., will be removed. Our wives and daughters will be able to walk in the woods at 2:00 a.m. and never have any fears. All the liars, adulterers, and those who make afraid will be gone.

Who among us, clothed with celestial bodies, and presided over by Christ and the prophets, with Satan and wickedness gone, could not learn to abide by the commandments in 1,000 years? We all can if we are willing to take the Holy Ghost as our guide in this life.

> *And at that day, when I shall come in my glory, shall the parable be fulfilled which I spake concerning the ten virgins. For they that are wise and have received the truth, and have taken the Holy Spirit for their guide, and have not been deceived . . . shall abide the day.* (D&C 45:56-57.)

President Marion G. Romney said:

Spirituality comes by faith, repentance, baptism, and reception of the Holy Ghost. One who has the companionship of the Holy Ghost is in harmony with God. He is, therefore, spiritual. Spirituality is sustained by so living as to keep that companionship. [10]

All of the effort to prepare ourselves to receive the gift of the celestial kingdom is worth it. Jesus Christ did ninety percent of all the work that is necessary to meet the demands of justice on our behalf. All we need to do is walk by the Spirit daily, and press forward. Does that give us hope? It should! If we feel the presence of the Spirit in our lives, the light of our hope should glow brighter.

---

10. Marion G. Romney, *Conference Report*, Oct. 1979, p. 20.

Chapter Two

How to Qualify for
The Celestial Kingdom

JESUS ASKS US TO enter the strait gate and the narrow way.

> *Enter ye in at the strait gate: for wide is the gate, and broad is the way, that leadeth to destruction, and many there be which go in thereat: Because strait is the gate, and narrow is the way, which leadeth unto life, and few there be that find it.* (Matt. 7:13–14; D&C 132:25.)

Question: The strait and narrow way leads to where?

Answer: Unto eternal life. (2 Nephi 31:18 or D&C 132:22.)

Question: What is meant by eternal life?

Answer: Eternal is another name for Heavenly Father. (D&C 19:10–11.) Therefore, eternal life means God's life or to live with God and have eternal increase. (D&C 132:20.) Nephi instructs us on how to enter the strait and narrow path:

> *Wherefore, do the things which I have told you I have seen that your Lord and your Redeemer should do; for, for this cause have they been shown unto me, that ye might know the gate by which ye should enter.* **For the gate by which ye should enter is repentance and**

baptism by water; and then cometh a remission of your sins by fire and by the Holy Ghost.

And then are ye in this strait and narrow path which leads to eternal life; *yea, ye have entered in by the gate; ye have done according to the commandments of the Father and the Son; and ye have received the Holy Ghost, which witnesses of the Father and the Son, unto the fulfilling of the promise which he hath made, that if ye entered in by the way ye should receive.*

And now, my beloved brethren, after ye have gotten into this strait and narrow path, I would ask if all is done? Behold I say unto you, Nay; for ye have not come thus far save it were by the word of Christ with unshaken faith in him, relying wholly upon the merits of him who is mighty to save.

Wherefore, ye must press forward with a steadfastness in Christ, having a perfect brightness of hope, and a love of God and of all men. Wherefore, if ye shall press forward, feasting upon the word of Christ, and endure to the end, behold, thus saith the Father: Ye shall have eternal life.

And now, behold, my beloved brethren, this is the way; and there is none other way nor name given under heaven whereby man can be saved in the kingdom of God. And now, behold, this is the doctrine of Christ, and the only and true doctrine of the Father, and of the Son, and of the Holy Ghost, which is one God, without end. Amen. (2 Nephi 31:17-21.) *(Emphasis added)*

Question: What must one do to enter the strait and narrow path?

Answer: 1. One must have faith in the Lord Jesus Christ. (John 14:6.)

2. One must repent of his sins. (2 Nephi 31:17.)

3. One must be baptized by water. (2 Nephi 31:17.)

Question: What gift does one receive after entering the strait and narrow path?

Answer: The gift of the Holy Ghost. (2 Nephi 31:18.)

Question: What does the Holy Ghost do for us?

Answer: He cleanses us of our sins. (2 Nephi 31:17.) We become spiritually born again.

Born Again (a spiritual rebirth)

One is born into mortality when he becomes alive physically. To have "spiritually been born of God" means that one has become alive to things of the Spirit. Alma says, "A mighty change was also wrought in their hearts, and they humbled themselves and put their trust in the true and living God." (Alma 5:13.) This person now recognizes God and his Son Jesus Christ. He seeks to follow their ways, laws, ordinances, and commandments. He seeks counsel daily from heaven. He sees that which is going on in the temporal world through his spiritual eyes. His perspective of life is seen in the eternal dimension. The Holy Ghost is his constant companion (D&C 121:46.) and he experiences the fruits of the Spirit—love, joy, peace, longsuffering, gentleness, goodness, faith, meekness, and temperance. (Galatians 5:22-23.) Bruce R. McConkie says:

> Mere compliance with the formality of the ordinance of baptism does not mean that a person has been born again...the new birth takes place only for those who actually enjoy the gift or companionship of the Holy Ghost, only for those who are fully converted, who have given themselves without restraint to the Lord. [1]

Question: One becomes a candidate for which kingdom once he enters the strait and narrow path?

Answer: Celestial kingdom.

Please note the following. Elder McConkie explains the strait and narrow path:

> To enter at the strait gate is to forsake the world, repent of one's sins, and be baptized under the hands of a legal administrator, thus getting on the straight and narrow path which leads to eternal life. The strait gate opens the door or gate to the kingdom of God on earth

---

1. Bruce R. McConkie, *Mormon Doctrine*, p. 101.

(which is the Church) and to the kingdom of God in
heaven (which is the celestial kingdom). [2]

Joseph Fielding Smith said:

I have been asked quite a number of times by members
of the Church if baptism would permit a person to enter
the celestial kingdom. Each time I have been astonished
that any member of the Church would ask that question
after all that has been written and the words of the Savior
himself. When he sent his disciples out after his
resurrection he said, they who repent and believe and are
baptized should be saved, and they who would not repent
and would not be baptized should not be saved. That is the
doctrine the Lord has given to the Church in our day.

Who among us wants to be satisfied by merely entering
in the celestial kingdom? The Lord did not say that
baptism would exalt us. Are we going to be satisfied with
merely an entrance? Evidently there are many members
of the Church who are going to be so satisfied, because
they will not prepare themselves, or do not prepare to
receive the exaltation. What will happen to those who are
baptized, who are satisfied thus far? They will enter into
that kingdom to be servants, to wait upon those who are
worthy of a far more and exceeding weight of glory. The
Lord says they will be angels, ministering servants, but
they will not be Gods, and that will be their destiny, for he
says it will endure worlds without end. So we cannot be
satisfied merely with baptism. The Lord expects us to be
worthy to go on and receive the fulness of his kingdom, to
be clothed with the power of perfection and become like
him. That can only be done by observing the ordinances
and receiving the covenants in the house of the Lord, each
of us individually and for our dead. We must perform
these like services for them. [3]

---

2. Ibid., p. 769.
3. Joseph Fielding Smith, *Seek Ye Earnestly*, (Deseret Book, 1970,) p. 62.

Conclusion

If one has submitted to the ordinances that Jesus commanded and has experienced a spiritual rebirth, then one is cleansed from the sins of this generation and becomes a candidate for the celestial kingdom TODAY.

Questions:	**Yes**	**No**
1. Have you accepted Jesus as the Christ?	☐	☐
2. Have you repented of your sins?	☐	☐
3. Have you been baptized by those having authority?	☐	☐
4. Have you received the gift of the Holy Ghost?	☐	☐
5. Have you spiritually been born of God?	☐	☐

If you answered yes to all five questions then you are in the strait and narrow path that leads to exaltation. You are a candidate for the celestial kingdom and if the Savior came today you would be lifted up to meet him. Knowing these things should greatly increase our hope.

Chapter Three

Answers to
Celestial Kingdom Questions

BUT, DON'T I HAVE TO be *perfect* before I can receive a celestial body?

Answer: No, just clean and progressing spiritually. There are three levels in the celestial glory — if a person had to be perfect in order to enter, there would be no need for three different levels. For example, a seven-year old can lie, cheat, steal, and kick his little sister, and die before the age eight and still inherit the highest degree in the celestial kingdom. Why? Because he is clean. He cannot sin until the age of eight. He transgressed some laws but because of Jesus Christ's sacrifice, he is clean, worthy to enter into exaltation.

> Little children shall be saved. They are alive in Christ and shall have eternal life. For them the family unit will continue, and the fulness of exaltation is theirs. No blessing shall be withheld. They shall rise in immortal glory, grow to full maturity, and live forever in the highest heaven of the celestial kingdom.... [1]

Brigham Young responds to this question as follows:

> If a person with an honest heart, a broken, contrite, and pure spirit, in all fervency and honesty of soul, presents himself and says that he wishes to be baptized for the remission of his sins, and the ordinance is administered by one having authority, is that man saved? Yes, to that period of time. Should the Lord see proper to take him then from the earth, the man has believed and been baptized, and is a fit subject for heaven — a candidate for the kingdom of God in the celestial world, because he has repented and done all that was required of him in that hour. [2]

Question: But, don't I have to be perfect *before* I can be assured exaltation?

Answer: Elder McConkie answered this question. He first quotes 2 Nephi 31:20, then says the following:

> All the faithful Saints, all of those who have endured to the end, depart this life with the absolute guarantee of eternal life.
>
> There is no equivocation, no doubt, no uncertainty in our minds. Those who have been true and faithful in this life will not fall by the wayside in the life to come. If they keep their covenants here and now and depart this life firm and true in the testimony of our blessed Lord, they shall come forth with an inheritance of eternal life.
>
> We do not mean to say that those who die in the Lord, and who are true and faithful in this life, must be perfect in all things when they go into the next sphere of existence. There was only one perfect man, the Lord Jesus, whose Father was God.
>
> ... But what we are saying is that when the saints of God chart a course of righteousness, when they gain sure testimonies of the truth and divinity of the Lord's work,

---

1. Bruce R. McConkie, *Ensign,* April 1977, p. 3.
2. Brigham Young, *Journal of Discourses,* 8:124.

when they keep the commandments, when they overcome the world, when they put first in their lives the things of God's kingdom, when they do all these things, and then depart this life though they have not yet become perfect they shall nevertheless gain eternal life in our Father's kingdom; and eventually they shall be perfect as God their Father and Christ His Son are perfect. [3]

Question: What does it mean to be perfect?

Joseph Fielding Smith gives us some insight into Matthew 5:48, "Be ye therefore perfect, even as your Father which is in heaven is perfect":

Salvation does not come all at once; we are commanded to be perfect even as our Father in heaven is perfect. It will take ages to accomplish this end, for there will be greater progress beyond the grave, and it will be there that the faithful will overcome all things, and receive all things, even the fulness of the Father's glory.

I believe the Lord means just what he said: that we should be perfect, as our Father in heaven is perfect. That will not come all at once, but line upon line, and precept upon precept, example upon example, and even then not as long as we live in this mortal life, for we will have to go even beyond the grave before we reach that perfection and shall be like God. [4]

Bruce R. McConkie suggests a definition for two kinds of perfection.

1) **Finite or mortal perfection** — It consists in living a godfearing life of devotion to the truth, of walking in complete submission to the will of the Lord, and of putting first in one's life the things of the kingdom of God.

2) **Infinite perfection** — is reserved for those who overcome all things and inherit the fulness of the Father

---

3. Bruce R. McConkie, *Ensign*, Nov. 1976, p. 107.
4. Joseph Fielding Smith, *Doctrines of Salvation*, 2:18.

in the mansions hereafter. It consists in gaining eternal life, the kind of life which God has in the highest heaven within the celestial world. [5]

Joseph Smith defines the perfect person as one who has acquired all the attributes of God to the degree he has developed them. Some of these attributes are: knowledge of all things, faith or power, justice, righteous judgments, mercy, and truth. Because of these attributes, man can exercise faith in God and thereby remove doubt and gain eternal life. [6]

Bruce R. McConkie indicates that Jesus didn't receive infinite perfection until he received all power in heaven and earth, which was given to him after his resurrection. He also indicates that the "attainment of infinite perfection includes the acquisition of all the attributes of godliness in their fulness, so a person who is perfect, as the Father is perfect, has also gained the same degree of mercy possessed by Deity." [7]

Our focus needs to be on spiritual progression rather than perfection. We will become like God, for we love him and want to be like him. However, for now, I will concentrate on overcoming the world by learning and applying the gospel in my life and seeking the guidance of my Father in Heaven.

Question: Does one become perfect overnight?

Answer: "And he received not of the fulness at first, but continued from grace to grace, until he received a fulness; And thus He was called the Son of God because he received not of the fulness at the first." (D&C 93:13-14.)

Question: Am I justified if I am on the road to perfection and progressing?

Answer: Joseph Fielding Smith has answered this question:

---

5. Bruce R. McConkie, *Mormon Doctrine*, p. 567.

6. *Lectures on Faith*, pp. 41–48.

7. Bruce R. McConkie, *Doctrinal New Testament Commentary*, (Bookcraft,) 1:231.

It is our duty to be better today than we were yesterday, and better tomorrow than we are today. Why? Because we are on that road, if we are keeping the commandments of the Lord, we are on that road to perfection, and that can only come through obedience and the desire in our hearts to overcome the world. [8]

Question: How can one tell if his level of spiritual performance is acceptable to God?

Answer: What then is the law of justification? It is simply this: "All covenants, contracts, bonds, obligations, oaths, vows, performances, connections, associations, or expectations" (D&C 132:7.), in which men must abide to be saved and exalted, must be entered into and performed in righteousness so that the Holy Spirit can justify the candidate for salvation....

We know when something is justified because the Spirit will be with us. The companionship of the Spirit, graciously extended by the Lord, is the witness or evidence of justification. [9]

Question: What does it mean to be saved or to gain one's salvation?

Answer: Elder McConkie in *Mormon Doctrine* says the following about the highest level of salvation:

Salvation in its true and full meaning is synonymous with exaltation or eternal life and consists in gaining an inheritance in the highest of the three heavens within the celestial kingdom. With few exceptions this is the salvation of which the scriptures speak. It is the salvation which saints seek. It is of this which the Lord says, "There is no gift greater than the gift of salvation." (D&C 6:13.) This full salvation is obtained in and through the continuation of the family unit in eternity, and those who obtain it are gods. (D&C 131:1-4; 132.) [10]

---

8. Joseph Fielding Smith, *Doctrines of Salvation,* 2:18–19.

9. *Melchizedek Priesthood Study Guide,* 1978–79, p. 46.

10. Bruce R. McConkie, *Mormon Doctrine, p. 670.*

Joseph Fielding Smith expands the meaning of salvation:

Redemption according to the gospel, is the gift of God to every creature born into the world, that he shall live again, being entitled to the resurrection. Christ is frequently spoken of in the scriptures as our Redeemer, and so refers to himself.

Salvation is the gift of God, according to the scriptures, to all men who do not sin against the light and become sons of perdition. Salvation is of varying stages or degrees. Every man is to be judged according to his works, and for this reason various degrees or kingdoms have been established.

Exaltation is to dwell in the presence of God and to be like him. [11]

Question: How long is enduring to the end?

This question arises from scriptures like 2 Nephi 31:20 in which Nephi has told us how to enter the strait and narrow path that leads to eternal life, and then in order for us to continue in that path he says:

Wherefore, ye must press forward with a steadfastness in Christ, having a perfect brightness of hope, and a love of God and of all men. Wherefore, if ye shall press forward, feasting upon the words of Christ, and **endure to the end,** *behold thus saith the Father: Ye shall have eternal life.*

Answer: Elder McConkie answers:

Baptism is the gate which puts the converted Christian on the straight and narrow path which leads to eternal life. To gain the promised inheritance in the celestial world it is necessary to travel the length of the path, a course of travel which consists in obedience to the laws and principles of the gospel. This process is called enduring to the end, meaning the end of mortal life. [12]

---

11. Joseph Fielding Smith, *Doctrines of Salvation,* 2:13.

12. Bruce R. McConkie, *Mormon Doctrine,* p. 228.

Question: What do you mean, *qualify* for the celestial kingdom? I thought I had to *earn* a place in the celestial kingdom?

Answer: The celestial kingdom is a gift.

> *If thou wilt do good, yea, and hold out faithful to the end, thou shalt be saved in the kingdom of God, which is the greatest of all the* **gifts** *of God; for there is no gift greater than the* **gift of salvation**. (D&C 6:13.)

> *For by grace are ye saved through faith; and that not of yourselves: it is the* **gift of God**. (Ephesians 2:8.)

> *For we labor diligently to write, to persuade our children, and also our brethren, to believe in Christ, and to be reconciled to God; for we know that it is by grace that we are saved, after all we can do.* (2 Nephi 25:23.)

Jesus Christ has paid the price for us to enter the celestial kingdom. If one qualifies, he will receive this gift free; he does not earn this gift. However, he must make the effort to qualify to prepare himself to enjoy the gift. To illustrate, let us assume you have made application to a university for a scholarship. The scholarship will pay you $2,000 per year for four years. Must you earn the scholarship of $2,000? Definitely not. The money has already been earned by someone else. It would be a gift to you. However, you must qualify in order to be considered for the scholarship. You must:

1) Graduate from high school.
2) Maintain a "B" average in the past twelve months of school.
3) Have leadership experience.
4) Be recommended by your bishop.
5) Be willing to live the school standards.
6) Be willing to major in a specific field at college.
7) Make application for the scholarship.

As you can see, it does take work and effort to prepare for the scholarship. By the same token, it takes work and effort to qualify for the gift of the celestial kingdom. It takes effort to gain sufficient faith in Jesus Christ, to pray, study and attend church.

It takes time and effort to repent of one's sins, and then be baptized.

We should note that the work and effort to qualify for the gift is not equal to the gift. For example, if your last name were Rockefeller, some day you might inherit millions of dollars as long as you were qualified. That is, if you followed the family's traditions by attending certain schools, setting the proper example in the community, and had a similar philosophy as espoused by the Rockefellers, you might be eligible for an inheritance. However, your best friend could attend the same schools, be an example in the community, and have the same philosophy as you, but he would not be eligible for these millions of dollars. Why? To you the money is a gift for which you may qualify. To your friend, on the other hand, that much money would have to be earned dollar by dollar. The potential gift to you is much greater than the work and effort you expend to qualify for it.

Satan desires to discourage us; therefore he teaches us that we must earn the celestial kingdom. This is a lie. What could we possibly do to earn billions of dollars in this life, let alone the celestial kingdom? We do not earn the celestial kingdom, for we know it is a gift, freely given to all who will make application, be baptized, and then press forward.

One day a non-Mormon said, "The problem with the LDS Church is that you are 'Indian-givers.' You give a gift to someone, like salvation, and then you take it back and say one has to earn it; therefore, it is not free."

I asked him, "Do I need to accept Christ to be saved?"

He answered, "Yes."

"Does one have to repent of his sins in order to be saved, or can one continue to sin?" I continued.

He said, "One needs to repent of his sins."

I then asked if one needed to try to keep the Ten Commandments in order to be saved, and he answered, "Yes, one should try to keep the commandments." He looked surprised, realizing that he had just said that salvation was indeed free, but that one had to qualify for that gift by obedience or it would have no value to him.

> *For what doth it profit a man if a gift is bestowed upon him, and he receives not the gift? Behold, he rejoices not in that which is given unto him, neither rejoices in him who is the giver of the gift.* (D&C 88:33.)

What value would the gift of a new car be to my daughter if she did not know how to drive and had no desire to learn? The gift would have no value to her except to sell for money. Now, suppose I promised her great blessings in her life if she would pay the necessary price to learn how to drive, if she would give up some of her time to study, if she would promise to live by the rules of the land, and if she would go through the embarrassment of learning how to drive, making mistakes, correcting them, etc. Now, if my daughter would do these requirements, she would get a driver's license.

Let us assume that my daughter said, "Dad, I do not know if what you say is true, but you have never lied to me and you always have my interest at heart. Therefore, I will do as you suggest." She studied and passed the exam. She made her mistakes, and she corrected them; she went through the put-downs and the sly remarks of others. At last she attained her driver's license. Does the gift of the car now have value to her? Yes. Why? Because she put forth the necessary effort to be able to enjoy the gift. Did she earn the gift? No. I paid the thousands of dollars for the car; she did not earn a dollar of it. But, she put in the necessary work to qualify for the gift and therefore, is *able to enjoy it* and use it.

Christ has created the celestial kingdom and cleared the path for us to inherit that gift. But we need to put our lives in order (which does take effort and work) by repenting and keeping the necessary commandments in order to qualify for the gift and to be prepared to enjoy it.

Question: Let us assume that you have been baptized and received the Holy Ghost; at that moment you were clean and worthy for a celestial inheritance. But, how about today, now? How can you tell if you are still clean and worthy to inherit the celestial kingdom?

Answer: You can know by having the companionship of the Holy Ghost. If you are worthy to have the Holy Ghost in your life today, then you know that by God's standard you are still clean and, therefore, qualified for that glory. One cannot have the spiritual influences of the Holy Ghost and be unclean, according to Bruce R. McConkie:

> ... his sins are forgiven him, as witnessed by the fact that he receives the companionship of the Spirit, which he could not have if he were unworthy.
> ... they are rewarded with the companionship of the Spirit, which companionship they cannot have unless they are cleansed and purified from sin.
> It is an axiomatic gospel verity that the spirit of the Lord will not dwell in an unclean tabernacle. [13]

Question: Yes, but this sounds too easy.

Answer: One needs to keep in mind that there is a difference between receiving a celestial body and qualifying for exaltation. One cannot become perfect in this life, and thus one will use the time in the Millennium to receive the help needed to reach perfection or exaltation.

The key is to walk under the direction of the Holy Ghost daily. As long as we do this we are in the strait and narrow path that leads to eternal life. We need to follow the counsel of President Heber J. Grant:

---

13. Bruce R. McConkie, *Doctrinal New Testament Commentary*, 3:275.

I do not believe that any man lives up to his ideals, but if we are striving, if we are working, if we are trying, to the best of our ability, to improve day by day, then we are in the line of our duty. If we are seeking to remedy our own defects, if we are so living that we can ask God for light, for knowledge, for intelligence, and above all, for His Spirit, that we may overcome our weaknesses, then, I can tell you, we are in the straight and narrow path that leads to life eternal. Then we need have no fear.[14]

One cannot walk with a member of the Godhead and not improve daily. To qualify for the gift of becoming clean, one must have faith, must repent, and must be baptized; then he becomes a candidate for the celestial kingdom. And, as long as he walks in the strait and narrow path each day, he is still a candidate for celestial glory.

The next step is to "press forward," to continue to gain more light, and then to live by it so that one may receive still further light until at last one receives a fulness of light.

> *That which is of God is light; and he that receiveth light, and continueth in God, receiveth more light; and that light groweth brighter and brighter until the perfect day.* (D&C 50:24.)

How does one "continue in God"? He does this by walking under the direction of the Holy Ghost.

Question: How do I know that I am walking in the strait and narrow path daily?

Answer: First, by feeling the influence of the Holy Ghost in your life each day. Remember, the more you feel the love of God, the more you will feel love for others and peace within yourself. And this perfect love cometh through the power of the Holy Ghost. (Moroni 8:26.)

Second, by doing strait-and-narrow-path works out of the love you feel for God and Jesus Christ, and not out of a need to prove

---

14. Heber J. Grant, *Gospel Standards*, (Bookcraft, 1944,) pp. 184–85.

your worth, or to out-do someone else.

Question: What is strait-and-narrow-path work?

Answer: Attending priesthood meeting, doing home teaching, blessing the sick, holding family home evening, and doing temple work would be good examples. But so would changing diapers, washing dishes, mowing lawns, paying bills, sleeping, playing with the children, and exercising. The above activities can affect one's spiritual growth, therefore, the necessary attention must be given to each in order to stay in the strait and narrow path.

Question: Is it possible for a member of the Church to feel he is ready to meet the Savior each and every day?

Answer: Yes, by feeling the influence of the Holy Ghost in one's life daily, one can know that he is ready to meet the Savior. Brigham Young has said:

> It is present salvation and the present influence of the Holy Ghost that we need every day to keep us on saving ground...if he had continued in righteousness and obedience to the requirements of heaven, he is saved all the time, through baptism, the laying on of hands, and obeying the commandments of the Lord and all that is required of him by the heavens—the living oracles. He is saved now, next week, next year, and continually, and is prepared for the celestial kingdom of God whenever the time comes for him to inherit it. [15]

And President Lorenzo Snow said:

> All men and women who are worthy to be called Latter-day Saints should live hour by hour in such a way that if they should be called suddenly from this life into the next they would be prepared. The preparation should be such that we should not fear to be called away suddenly into the Spirit Life. It is our privilege to so live as to have the spirit of light and intelligence to that extent that we shall

15. Brigham Young, *Journal of Discourses*, 8:124.

feel satisfied that all will be well if we should be called away at any hour. [16]

Question: Yes, but how about all the commandments, laws, ordinances, and suggestions that I am supposed to keep and do not?

Answer: One's light and knowledge always stays ahead of one's works. You will always have more light than you are presently living. This fact of life was by design. It looks like this:

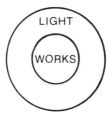

As a person increases his works, his light will also increase. It seems that God allows us to know more than we are presently living. He shows us a few of our weaknesses so we can have hope in overcoming them. If he showed us all of our inadequacies at once we would be devastated. As we overcome some of our faults, our light grows and we see additional areas that can be improved.

Now, some people use this fact of life to condemn themselves. They conclude that they need not study the gospel, for they already know more than they are living. They conclude that since they never seem to be able to live up to their light fully, that they should not try. They assume that other people live up to their light, and that they are the only ones who do not. Such reasoning is self-defeating and is from Satan. It diminishes their hope—and as we have seen, we each have ample reason to retain hope in our own exaltation.

---

16. Lorenzo Snow, *Conference Report,* Oct. 1899, p. 2.

ASSIGNMENT

President Heber J. Grant suggests we fulfill the following assignment:

> The all-important thing for you and me is to discover whether we are walking in the straight and narrow path that leads to life eternal, and if we are not, wherein have we allowed the adversary to blind our minds and to cause us to depart from that path which will lead us back into the presence of God? Each one should search his own heart to find out wherein he has failed, and then he should diligently seek our Heavenly Father for the assistance of His Holy Spirit, that he may come back into the straight path. By the assistance of our Heavenly Father there is no obligation and no law in the Church that we cannot fulfill. The Lord will give us the strength and the ability to accomplish every duty and labor that rests upon us in an acceptable manner in his sight. The only quest is, have we the disposition?

Let us follow President Grant's suggestion; **If I am not sure whether I am in the strait and narrow path,** I will put in writing exactly what is required of me to get on that path today, according to the scriptures and the prophets, so I can feel the influence of the Holy Ghost.

And **for those who do feel the influence of the Holy Ghost in their lives,** and therefor are candidates for the Celestial Kingdom, and are qualified to meet the Savior, will proceed as follows. I will seek to feel that power each day so my hope of being raised up to meet the Savior will grow stronger and stronger, until I have that perfect brightness of hope.

Section II

LOVE GOD AND ALL MEN

In Section I, we reviewed what is required to enter the strait and narrow path, to become candidates for the celestial kingdom. We understand now that we are candidates, qualified to receive celestial bodies when the time comes for that inheritance. We know we have much to do in order to become like our Heavenly Parents, but we know that we have this life plus 1,000 years in the Millennium to accomplish this. Our "brightness of hope" has increased in the fact that each of us can and will qualify for this great gift of eternal life.

Once we are on the strait and narrow path, what must we do next? Nephi asked that very question: "And now, my beloved brethren, after ye have gotten into this strait and narrow path, I would ask if all is done?" Then he answers,

> *I say unto you, NAY; . . . wherefore, ye must press forward with a steadfastness in Christ, having a perfect brightness of hope, and a love of God and of all men. Wherefore, if ye shall press forward, feasting upon the word of Christ, and endure to the end, behold, thus saith the Father: Ye shall have eternal life.* (2 Nephi 31:19–20.)

Our goal now is to develop a "perfect brightness of hope," which will remove all doubt and allow us to focus all our energies on keeping the first and great commandment of loving God with all our hearts, souls, strength, and minds. (Luke 10:25-29.)

Nephi suggests that in order for each of us to gain eternal life, we need to develop genuine feelings of love for God and all men. We are also counseled to have unconditional love for ourselves. This section will review this law and how we can have joy as we progress in the strait and narrow path toward eternal life, and how we can make dominant in our lives these feelings of love for Heavenly Father.

Chapter Four

This Pure Love of Christ

A LAWYER ASKED JESUS:

> *Master, which is the great commandment in the law?*
> *Jesus said unto him, Thou shalt love the Lord thy God with all thy heart, and with all thy soul, and with all thy mind.*
> *This is the first and great commandment. And the second is like unto it. Thou shalt love thy neighbour as thyself.*
> *On these two commandments hang all the law and the prophets.*
> (Matthew 22:35–40.)

The Savior taught the lawyer several principles. *First*, we are to love God with all our heart, soul, and mind. *Second*, we are to love our neighbors. *Third*, we are to feel love for ourselves. *Fourth*, all the other laws, ordinances, and commandments are of little value unless we are in possession of the emotion of love for God — this pure love of Christ. What does it mean to love God with all our heart, soul, might, mind, and strength?

Bruce R. McConkie suggests the following:

> *All thy heart* with perfect sincerity and uprightness, not dividing one's devotion, but having it centered totally in Deity.
>
> *All thy soul* with utmost fervor . . . thus love is to come from the whole being, from the inner man as well as the temporal being.
>
> *All thy mind* with intelligence and sense as distinguished from blind and unthinking devotion; with enlightened reason as distinguished from mystical and incomprehensible worship.
>
> *All thy strength* with might, power, and intensity; with all the energy of one's being. [1]

To love God with all one's heart means that his feelings for him would transcend all other emotions, temporal conditions, and human relationships. For example:

1. Though rejected by others, one's feelings of love would be greater than his feelings of rejection; his need for other's approval to feel worth would be secondary to his need to share the love he felt for God.

2. One would hate no one. To hate someone would put feelings of hate above feelings of love. One cannot love God and feel hate for his brother. (1 John 4:20-21.) In order to hate anyone one must set his love for God aside.

3. When one is afraid to share the gospel with strangers, his fear is greater than his love of God, because "perfect love casteth out fear." (1 John 4:18.) How might one overcome this fear? Only by drawing closer to God and enlarging his capacity to feel the pure love of God until it extends to strangers.

4. When one is fired from his job, he would turn unto God for strength, for his feelings for God are greater than the emotions created from losing the job. (Alma 26:12.)

---

1. Bruce R. McConkie, *Doctrinal New Testament Commentary,* 1:610.

5. When one's teenaged son or daughter is in trouble at school, at church, or with the law, his feelings of social embarrassment are transcended by his feelings of love for God and his child.

6. When one does home teaching, visiting teaching or teaches a Sunday School lesson, it is done out of the love he feels for God. It is done for Him and for the gratitude felt for His sacrifice. It is not done to gain social acceptance or for ego satisfaction. (John 12:43.)

7. Service in the Church is not done out of duty or obligation or even out of a desire to serve one's fellowman. (2 Corinthians 9:6-8.) It is done out of this pure love of Christ. Therefore, when one's fellows (even in the Church — home teaching, Sunday School class, MIA, or Primary group) reject him, he will remain steadfast in Christ and still feel love for them.

8. For one to love God with all his heart, means that one takes care of his physical body, his mental development, his spiritual growth, and his temporal assets *with God in mind.*

9. One would seek the Lord's counsel, looking to him in every thought. (D&C 6:36.) This would not be a burden, but an opportunity to have God contribute to one's success. God charges no temporal fee for his counsel, directions, or participation. He is always right; he really cares that every one of us succeeds, and he is *always* available.

10. When one sins, his knowledge of God's love would help draw him back into the strait and narrow path. It is Satan who would tell him that God doesn't love him anymore because of his mistake. But this person would reject Satan's lie, for he knows that God *does* care and has great love for him, even though he cannot feel God's love at the moment. (Alma 5:33, Ephesians 2:4-5.)

11. One would not condemn himself when he makes mistakes or doesn't accomplish all the things he knows should be done. Such self-condemnation removes one from feeling the pure love of Christ. When one fails, he should look to God for

strength to improve, rather than spend his energy in self-condemnation, contrary to the gospel of Jesus Christ.

12. When one strives to keep the commandments, he draws closer to God, and his feelings of charity expand. He does not seek to keep the commandments out of feelings of guilt, or to feel accepted by his fellowman out of feelings of duty or obligation. (2 Corinthians 9:6-8.)

13. His feelings of love will dominate all worldly praise, money, honors, or anything else found in this world. (1 John 2:15.)

14. This love for God will be stronger than any love he feels for friends, parents, spouse, or children. (Matthew 10:37.)

Dominating Emotions Determine One's Actions

There are times when our feelings for God dominate our lives, and we feel great peace and joy with Him, with our fellowman, and with ourselves. There are other times when the cares of this world become dominant, and it is hard to let feelings of charity preside. Developing a pure love of Christ takes time, effort, and concentration. The primary purpose of this book is to help each of us find ways to grow in this perfect love of God.

Some people assume that they do not have the pure love of Christ because this emotion does not dominate their lives each moment of the day. But the real question to ask is "Am I improving, because I choose to draw to him daily?"

Remember that dominating emotions will determine our actions for the current moment of time. For example, a young man came to my home one day to give me his temple recommend. It seems that he had argued with his boss over something the boss had done to him, and he had lost the Spirit. He felt that he was no longer worthy to hold a temple recommend.

That morning he and his family had family prayer. His feelings for Heavenly Father had been strong. He felt good about his life, family, and what the day would hold for him. After he arrived at work a couple of things went wrong which had upset him, but he stayed in control. Had someone asked him about the Church, he would have gladly testified of the gospel; he would have felt spiritually in tune. But during the morning the boss made some schedule changes without consulting him. Somewhat upset, the young man had gone to his employer's office to complain. His employer listened to him explain how offended he was, and how it was embarrassing to him when his co-workers knew what was going on before he did. As he warmed to his hurts, he made it clear that since he was in charge of this phase of the work, he would appreciate his employer's consulting him prior to making changes in his schedule.

Perhaps had the event ended at this point, all would have been fine, but his employer was now offended and abruptly expressed his authority, plus his concern about how effective my friend was in his job. At this point, my friend hit the ceiling emotionally. His feelings for Heavenly Father did not dominate his heart at all. In fact, these special feelings were nowhere in sight. The fault-finding of the boss created emotions in him at that moment that were much stronger than his feelings for Heavenly Father.

My young friend proceeded to tell the boss a thing or two. He swore at him, told him that others felt the same way he did about him, and said a few other bitter, mean things that came into his mind. Then he walked out, slammed the door, and went back to his duties.

One has to keep feeding emotions in order to maintain them. Some of the other employees had heard the confrontation; they wanted to know what had happened. My friend told his side of the story over and over. He really fed his negative emotions. In fact, it was after lunch before everyone had heard what had happened.

As the afternoon went by, our friend turned his mind and heart to his work and the intensity of his negative emotions began to diminish. By the time he climbed into his car to drive home, his negative feelings were reduced to the point that they were equal in intensity to his feelings about Heavenly Father. He wondered why he had been so dumb—why he had lost control and said things which weren't appropriate for an elder in the Church of Jesus Christ to say. When he arrived home and told his wife what had happened, his feelings for God were dominant again, and he felt very bad about his actions. He recognized that the Spirit was gone from him and he wondered if God could ever forgive him. It was then that he decided he wasn't worthy to hold a temple recommend and that he ought to see his stake president, who was just up the street.

I gave his recommend back to him. I told him that Heavenly Father loves him even when he makes mistakes. I told him that he needed to apologize to his employer for his actions and express these feelings to the other employees. He said that he would, but then asked, "Why do I do these things when I know better?" I explained the principle of dominating emotions, and that as he went about his daily activities, his feelings for God dominated his actions. But occasionally, a condition might arise that would create powerful emotions in him which he might choose over his love of God, and which would determine ungodly actions. However, as he turned away from these ungodly emotions and continued to draw closer to God, his feeling for Him would enlarge, and the day would finally come that his feelings of love for Heavenly Father would be so strong that no conditions or circumstances could create emotions that would be greater. His feeling of love for the Lord would dominate his life, and he would have overcome the world. I assured him that Heavenly Father would have patience with him as he progressed toward this great level of achievement.

What is the highest manifestation of love?

Devotion to one's fellowman, for when one is in the service of man he is in the service of God. (Mosiah 2:17.)

Yet, this statement isn't entirely true, for one can love his fellowman and not his God, but one cannot love God without loving and serving his fellowman. **The highest manifestation of love is devotion to God.** [2] Remember, however, that on this earth there are many good Christians who love Christ, and who serve their fellowman, yet will never see the celestial kingdom.

One who loves God will do his work. Temple work, missionary work, welfare work, ward and stake work, contributing time, money, and effort to the building of his kingdom on earth—one will do all of these things in God's ways, and not in his own way.

When one does home teaching, he will do it God's way. When members of a priesthood quorum were asked why they did home teaching, they replied with such answers as the following:

a. I feel better after it is done.

b. It is a priesthood assignment (obligation).

c. I enjoy visiting.

d. I enjoy hearing what the latest news is (gossip).

e. I have to do it (duty).

f. Because I love my families (serve fellowman).

g. I feel guilty if I don't do it.

h. I do not want to let my priesthood leaders down. (I do this assignment so my priesthood leaders will see me as a person of worth.)

i. Because I love my Heavenly Father and desire to serve him.

In actuality, every home teacher should seek to feel the love that God has for these families, and with these feelings of love go forth to teach. He will be sensitive to the Spirit as he carries out his assignment. He will depend upon God for inspiration as he develops a close relationship with these families.

---

2. Bruce R. McConkie, *Mormon Doctrine,* p. 459.

How does one manifest his love for another?

A daughter said to her father, "Now that I have a family, I certainly appreciate the time, effort, sacrifice, and love you have given me over the years. What can I do to repay you?"

How would you answer that question? Would you suggest that she and her husband pay you $400 per month for the rest of your life? Or do your yard work, or shine your shoes, or take you out to dinner? And even if she did these things, would it really repay you for all your efforts? Not likely.

This father told his daughter that the greatest gift she could give to him would be for her to love the Lord with all her heart and to serve Him unto exaltation. Why would this repay the father?

a. The daughter's spiritual growth, as she served God, would bring great joy into his heart and into hers because her capacity to feel this pure love of Christ would expand.

b. The daughter would experience the same love that the father had experienced in his sacrificing for her—which was the pure love of Christ. She would understand where her father's strength came from.

c. Both father and daughter would be able to have this feeling of joy together throughout eternity. They would understand each other; the love they have for each other would grow, drawing them closer to each other.

The father was repaid manyfold as his daughter served God and others. The daughter did nothing directly for her father, but he was greatly rewarded. The same principle applies to our repaying our Heavenly Father and his Son Jesus Christ for their love, sacrifice, and time spent in our behalf. We repay them by serving our fellowman and preparing ourselves to come back into God's presence. Out of the love we feel for God and his Son, each of us will grow into perfection and become like our Heavenly

Parents. For we will be like them, in love, justice, mercy, judgment, faith, truth, and knowledge.[3]

How does one manifest his love for God?

The scriptures admonish:

> *. . . by love serve one another.* (Galatians 5:13.)

> *Let all your things be done with charity.* (1 Corinthians 16:14.)

> *By this shall all men know that ye are my disciples, if ye have love one to another.* (John 13:35.)

> *If ye keep my commandments, ye shall abide in my love.* (John 15:10.)

We manifest our love for God by keeping his commandments (which enhances our spiritual growth), and by using the gift of charity in serving our fellowman. The focus is on serving one's fellowman out of the love one feels for Heavenly Father.

What is charity? Is it different from love for my fellowman?

> Charity is more than love, far more; it is everlasting love, perfect love, the pure love of Christ which endureth forever. It is love so centered in righteousness that the possessor has no aim or desire except for the eternal welfare of his own soul and for the souls of those around him.
>
> . . . no one can assist in the Lord's work without it (D&C 12:8, 18:19.); and the saints of God are commanded to seek and attain it. (D&C 121:45.) Charity is a gift of the Spirit which must be gained if one is to have salvation.[4]

God's love is perfect love; it is pure love; it is unconditional love; it is unfeigned love. As one seeks for this gift of the Spirit, he will be able to feel this pure love of Christ for himself, as well as for his neighbor.

---

3. Joseph Smith, *Lectures on Faith*, pp. 41–48.

4. Bruce R. McConkie, *Mormon Doctrine*, p. 121.

How does one get this gift of charity?

Charity comes by praying with all the energy of your heart unto God the Father that you will be filled with this love. (Moroni 7:48.) King Benjamin teaches that you can be filled with this love of God and obtain a remission of your sins if you always retain in your mind the greatness of God, his goodness, and his longsuffering towards you. (Mosiah 4:11-12.)

By using the gift of charity on behalf of others, our capacity for charity will expand.

What frame of mind must one have in order to receive this pure love of Christ?

a. One must have hope that he will be raised to eternal life. (Moroni 7:41.)

b. One must have faith in the Lord Jesus Christ—faith that Christ is the way to spiritual and temporal success. (Moroni 7:42.)

c. One must be meek and lowly of heart, that is, one must recognize his dependence upon God in all things. (Moroni 7:43.)

d. One must be spiritually alive to the degree that he can testify by the power of the Holy Ghost that Jesus is the Christ. (Moroni 7:44.)

What are the manifest qualities of one who has the pure love of Christ? (1 Corinthians 13.)

1. He suffereth long

- Out of this love one can suffer embarrassment of family members, teen-agers, or rejection by friends.
- Out of this love one may suffer in silence rather than point out the faults of others or try to get even.
- Out of this love one may give discipline to a child — even though as a consequence, the child's love may be willfully withdrawn.

2. Is Kind

- Feelings of tenderness and concern are always present even though discipline (firmness) is required.

3. Envieth not

- Because one sees all people through spiritual eyes, he can see that all persons have great spiritual worth. He becomes aware that temporal success is a condition of stewardship accountability, rather than a condition of worth.

4. Is not puffed up

- A person's feelings of self-worth are not tied to performance in the world or acceptance by the world. His strength is found in God and service to fellow beings. He gives, rather than takes.

5. Seeketh not his own

- Such a person wishes to serve Heavenly Father above all else.

6. Is not easily provoked

- His pure love of Christ is maintained with patience and forgiveness rather than with anger and condemned actions.

7. Thinketh no evil

- He seeks to have virtue garnish his thoughts unceasingly. (D&C 121:45–46.)

8. Rejoiceth not in iniquity but in truth

- He realizes that no one ever found happiness in wickedness.

9. Beareth all things

- He is not destroyed by rejection, put-downs, gossip, or persecution.

10. Believeth all things

- By the power of the Holy Ghost he may know the truth of all things.

11. Hopeth all things

- He maintains a perfect brightness of hope that he will be raised up to meet the Savior when he comes.

12. Endureth all things

- Yes, all. "He who loseth his life for my sake shall find it." (Matthew 10:39.)

What can separate a person like me from feeling the love of Christ?

a. Hating my neighbor, or my enemy, or my former spouse who has left me.

b. Being angry, or impatient.

c. Desiring position in the Church.

d. Nursing negative attitudes.

e. Disliking those who may criticize me and find fault with me.

f. Equating my worth as a child of God with my performance in mortality.

g. Allowing guilt feelings to control the heart.

h. Feeling hopeless—never feeling able to qualify for the celestial kingdom.

i. Putting anything above my loving God with all my heart.

j. Hating people who gave me wrong advice, financial or otherwise.

k. Remaining in sin.

The Apostle Paul asked:

> *Who shall separate us from the love of Christ? shall tribulation, or distress, or persecution, or famine, or nakedness, or peril, or sword? . . . nay, in all these things we are more than conquerors through him that loved us. For I am persuaded, that neither death, nor life, nor angels, nor principalities, nor powers, nor things present, nor things to come, nor heights, nor depth, nor any other creature, shall be able to*

separate us from the love of God, which is in Christ Jesus our Lord.
(Romans 8:35, 37–39.)

God *always* loves us; it is impossible to separate us from that love. But many things can separate us from a sense of that love in our lives, as well as a personal feeling of that love for God and for others. Our challenge, then, is to eliminate from our lives those elements that will diminish the love in our lives.

Chapter Five

Temporal and Spiritual Realities

IN ORDER FOR A PERSON to develop the pure love of Christ, he must understand the spiritual dimension where these feelings are understood, developed, and bestowed.

As one functions in this life, it is evident that there are two different dimensions of reality, and that each dimension operates under definite laws. For example, Alma and Amulek were cast into prison for preaching the gospel (Alma, chapter 14), and the rulers of Ammonihah demanded that all the wives and children of those men who believed the word of God should be cast into the fire. The rulers brought Alma and Amulek out of the prison to watch this horrible execution. When Amulek saw the agony of the women and little children in the flames, he cried out to Alma, "How can we witness this awful scene? Therefore let us stretch forth our hands, and exercise the power of God which is in us, and save them." But Alma replied calmly that the Spirit had told him that they should not do that, that the deaths of these innocents would stand in judgment against their destroyers, and that the suffering Saints were being received by the Lord unto His glory.

After this, Alma and Amulek were cast back into prison, and were not fed, or given water; their clothes were taken from them, and they were bound with strong cords; they were ridiculed, many came up to them and smote them, and many spit in their faces.

After many days of such treatment, Alma at last cried to God to give them strength according to their faith which was in Christ, and they broke their cords. Then the earth shook mightily, and the walls of the prison fell, crushing and killing those who were persecuting them.

> *And Alma and Amulek came forth out of the prison, and they were not hurt; for the Lord had granted unto them power, according to their faith which was in Christ.* (Alma 14:28.)

Alma and Amulek were imprisoned and suffered great emotional and physical pain inflicted by their enemies in the *temporal world,* but they found confidence and security and even peace in their persecution — and in the deaths of the women and the children — in the *spiritual dimension.*

In the *spiritual* dimension the power to do comes from God. Alma and Amulek called on God for spiritual power to break their cords, and for the powers of heaven to crush their prison walls. Their escape was based upon their faith in God and Jesus Christ. They exercised their spiritual senses. Had Alma and Amulek operated only in the temporal dimension, they would have exercised faith in themselves; they would have used their abilities (mental and physical) to escape. They would have dug a tunnel under the walls, or overpowered their guards, or waited until their friends came to free them.

If you had a daughter near death in the hospital, you would seek the Lord's help through mighty prayer and fasting. But if you restricted your efforts to the temporal dimension, you would seek the best doctors you could afford. You would study your daughter's sickness, give her suggested drugs, change her diet, and so on. You would show love to the daughter by being near her side day and night.

The temporal dimension is restricted by the physical world; the spiritual dimension is not restricted either by the physical world or mortality.

In order to act in the spiritual dimension, we need to open our minds and our hearts to God. There is no other way. In order to act in the spiritual dimension we need to have knowledge about this dimension, we need to know what is required of us and what we may expect. In order for you to use the powers of heaven to heal your daughter, you must be clean; you must be living the commandments sufficiently to be worthy of this grace, and you must have the authority or acknowledgment of God to act in his behalf. You must believe without doubt, or your faith will not be sufficient to open the doors of heaven. And when those great doors open, the spiritual dimension with all its powers and blessings will become available to you, just as real as are the sky and earth in the temporal dimension.

A babe, newly born into the world, learns about his temporal environment as he experiences it. He touches and watches and listens. He stuffs things into his mouth to find out how they taste. When he grows older, he will learn of more complicated things. He will learn suffering by suffering, and sin by sinning. In time, his experience in the temporal dimension may overwhelm his spiritual sensitivities.

> For what man knoweth the things of a man, save the spirit of man which is in him? even so the things of God knoweth no man, but the Spirit of God. . . . But the natural man receiveth not the things of the Spirit of God: for they are foolishness unto him: neither can he know them, because they are spiritually discerned. (1 Corinthians 2:11, 14.)

Because a natural man has never experienced the spiritual dimension, it ceases to exist for him.

But the spiritual dimension does exist, whether it is recognized or not. And it has no physical limitations. You might have a son or daughter on a mission in England or China, and, through the spiritual dimension, bring protection, love, and inspiration to them. You can cause the doors to open in far off countries to your missionary, and cause the rain to come or to stop, and the sun to hold its position, or great mountains to move. But in the temporal dimension you are limited to helping only those who are physically near to you, or who can be reached by phone, or mail.

In the Book of Mormon, Jacob defined truth, or reality, as "things as they really are, and of things as they really will be." He explains that the Spirit speaketh the truth and truth explains that which is real. (Jacob 4:13.) This concept that truth is only reality is repeated in the Doctrine and Covenants:

> And truth is knowledge of things as they are, and as they were, and as they are to come. (D&C 93:24.)

To perceive reality is to understand things as they really exist. One's mind can perceive and interpret spiritual realities as well as temporal realities. The scriptures are definite in recognizing that these two dimensions exist and are available to man.

> While we look not at things which are seen, but at the things which are not seen: for the things which are seen are temporal; but the things which are not seen are eternal. (2 Corinthians 4:18)

> And it came to pass that I said unto them that it was a representation of things both temporal and spiritual; . . . yea, even the works which were done by the temporal body. (1 Nephi 15:32)

> . . . asking for whatsoever things ye stand in need, both spiritual and temporal. (Alma 7:23)

> For by the power of my Spirit created I them; yea, all things both spiritual and temporal — First spiritual, secondly temporal, which is the beginning of my work; and again, first temporal, and secondly spiritual, which is the last of my work. (D&C 29:31, 32)

These two dimensions are meant to be mutually supportive; that is, they exist in a kind of partnership in which each enhances and enriches the other. Man, as he becomes aware, stands to benefit immeasurably, both temporally and spiritually, by the exchange.

For example, most of our experiences are in the physical world. It is in the physical world that we earn our living, raise our family, associate with others, and spend much time in eating, exercising, and being entertained. Yet each of us was sent to this world to overcome the world, (D&C 64:2.) to put it under our control along with the appetites, desires, and passions of mortality. (Alma 38:12.)

This great temporal assignment can best be done through using the spiritual dimension. For example, if a couple is experiencing great financial struggle, or perhaps deep family problems, they have two dimensions through which to seek solutions. They can probe the ways of the world and perhaps solve their problems through reason, study, and effort. Or they may seek additional help through the spiritual dimension and receive insight, and guidance, and spiritual strength to endure and overcome. Even though the difficulty may seem never completely solved, they will find meaning and purpose and strength against the temporal struggle from the spiritual dimension. And there are other benefits. They will come to a closeness with Heavenly Father, which will expand their spiritual insights and give them a peace which can be experienced only as they overcome the temporal through the spiritual.

It happens again and again. As one seeks for a testimony of his spiritual worth, he feels impressed to read the scriptures and pray about what the prophets have said. He begins to follow the scriptural admonitions and treat himself as a son or daughter of God. He then looks about himself and sees others around him as children of God. The result is a feeling of increased love and respect for himself and for others. His soul is filled; he sees everything more clearly, and the new perceptions and application in his life bring great joy to him. His life becomes more full, and his experiences become very delicious and precious to him.

Chapter Six

The Three Dimensions of Man

MAN HAS THREE integrated dimensions to his being. These are intellectual, physical, and spiritual. We must keep these in proper balance if we wish to develop God's love in our lives.

Man's intelligence is that part of him which has always existed. It was not created nor can it be. It is free to act and function within the sphere in which Heavenly Father has placed it. Intelligence is "light and truth." (D&C 93:29-30.) This dimension of man is free to choose good or evil, and each person is accountable for his choices. (Helaman 14:30-31.) This is the dimension that allows him to choose how he will feel, think, and act. "For the power is in them wherein they are agents unto themselves." (D&C 58:28.)

Man's spiritual dimension consists of man's intelligence clothed with a spiritual body. God is the Father of our spirits and so created them. (Hebrews 12:9; Numbers 16:22, 27:16.) This is the dimension of man that experiences deep feelings of love, tenderness, joy, peace, long-suffering, gentleness, meekness, temperance, and faith. (Galatians 5:22-23.) This dimension is nourished and grows through "giving of itself" through love, but it shrivels and atrophies through "taking," through selfishness, hatred, and contention. (Galatians 5:19-21.)

When one was born into earth life, his intelligence, clothed with a spiritual body, is integrated with a physical body into a unified, functioning system. The physical body has needs that must be provided for in order for it to maintain itself alive. Such things as food, rest, exercise, and warmth are necessary to its existence. These physical needs, along with other associated appetites, passions, and desires, can become exaggerated until they dominate the whole system, weakening and even destroying the intellectual and the spiritual. This is what has happened to people who are enslaved by their passions and wants, lusting out of control for such things as money, sex, food, drugs, or material possessions. But when a person meets the normal needs of the physical in normal balanced ways, his physical dimension provides pleasure and satisfaction.

The physical body is meant to be controlled by the spiritual. Physical appetites, passions, and desires are meant to work in harmony with the needs and strengths of the spirit. Both body and spirit are subject to the directing, independent power of the intelligence.

Dynamics of Man's Three Dimensions

Man needs food, exercise, rest, warmth, love, protection, and experience for his growth and well-being. The three dimensions of man provide these necessities. However, if one dimension is not allowed to function properly, then the basic needs of man are not satisfied and some type of disorder sets in. If the physical body is not fed, exercised, protected, and given proper rest, the whole man cannot function and will eventually die, even though he may be meditating spiritually twenty-four hours a day. If a person provides for his physical body at the expense of his spiritual body, his deep spiritual needs for love, goodness, kindness, tenderness, or acceptance will be neglected and will shrivel up and die. A spiritual deficiency develops within him, which he tries to meet through further physical action. But, of course, the physical body cannot satisfy spiritual needs. The body can only feel spirituality, the pure love of Christ, when it is in harmony with its spiritual dimension. As the intelligence of man keeps the proper balance between spiritual and physical, great growth, happiness, and peace prevails.

A modern prophet has said:

> There is another part of us, not so tangible, but quite as real as our physical body. This intangible part of us is described as mind, emotion, intellect, temperament, and many other things. Very seldom is it described as spiritual.
>
> But there is a spirit in man; to ignore it is to ignore reality. There are spiritual disorders, too, and spiritual diseases that can cause intense suffering.
>
> The body and the spirit of man are bound together. Often, very often, when there are disorders, it is very difficult to tell which is which.
>
> There are basic rules of physical health that have to do with rest, nourishment, exercise, and with abstaining from those things which damage the body. Those who violate the rules one day pay for their foolishness.
>
> There are also rules of spiritual health, simple rules that cannot be ignored, for if they are we will reap sorrow by and by.
>
> All of us experience some temporary physical sickness. All of us now and again may be spiritually ill as well. Too many of us, however, are chronically spiritually sick.
>
> We don't need to stay that way. We can learn to avoid spiritual infections and maintain good spiritual health. Even though we have a serious physical ailment, we can be spiritually healthy. [1]

1. Boyd K. Packer, *Conference Report*, Oct. 1977, p. 89.

The spiritual body needs to feel the pure love of Christ in order to grow and develop fully. As spiritual needs are met, one is better able to control and meet the needs of the physical body. By feeling the pure love of Christ, the individual will be better able to sense and express deep feelings of others. He will be able to feel deep respect for himself. He will be better able to handle rejection from others, as well as failure in the world.

A married couple who has all three dimensions in order will experience their love for each other through a sexual union which will be an expression of reverence, respect, and unity from deep within themselves. In contrast, if their physical appetites, passions, and desires dominate, and the spiritual aspects of their relationship are neglected, then their sexual union becomes a "taking" experience instead of a giving one, and the deep human needs each person has will go unmet. In time, unable or unwilling to repair their spiritual dimensions, these frustrated, unhappy people may seek to satisfy these deep, unmet needs with others, outside of their marriage. They seek, "for happiness in doing iniquity, which thing is contrary to the nature of that righteousness which is in our great and Eternal Head." (Helaman 13:38.)

The physical body alone cannot fill the deep spiritual needs for understanding, love, tenderness, and affectionate companionship. Without the spiritual dimension, a person cannot fully experience love and acceptance for others or for himself, let alone for Heavenly Father.

On the other hand, however, as one develops his spiritual feelings, he draws closer to the Holy Ghost. That member of the Godhead is assigned to help him grow spiritually, to subdue the lusts and wants of the flesh, and to develop, magnify, and purify all the natural passions and affections.

> The gift of the Holy Spirit adapts itself to all these organs or attributes. It quickens all the intellectual faculties, increases, enlarges, expands and purifies all the

natural passions and affections, and adapts them, by the gift of wisdom, to their lawful use. It inspires, develops, cultivates and matures all the fine toned sympathies, joys, tastes, kindred feelings and affections of our nature. It inspires virtue, kindness, goodness, tenderness, gentleness and charity. It develops beauty of person, form and features. It tends to health, vigor, animation and social feeling. It develops and invigorates all the faculties of the physical and intellectual man. It strengthens, invigorates and gives tone to the nerves. In short, it is, as it were, marrow to the bone, joy to the heart, light to the eyes, music to the ears, and life to the whole being. [2]

When man neglects the spiritual dimension, he cuts off that part of himself which can experience and share love, and joy, and peace. Sadly enough, he also cuts off that part of himself that can communicate with God, can feel God's love, and can be sensitive to his own deep feelings for himself. He becomes alone, separated from God, others, and even himself. This alienation occurs through spiritual neglect, or by treating oneself in ways contrary to one's true nature. When one recognizes his true worth as a son or daughter of God, born and reared in the courts of glory by Heavenly Parents, then he will act in ways that match this true identity, and these actions will facilitate growth and development of all three of his dimensions. But when one acts contrary to that real identity, he becomes alienated from others and from himself; this brings about frustration, anxiety, conflict, and eventually physical, spiritual, and intellectual sickness.

For example, if a person stimulates his physical appetites, passions, and desires through pornography, he is acting contrary to his real identity — his actions are offensive to his spiritual development. As he participates more and more in pornographic things, his spiritual dimension atrophies, and his need for love, tenderness, and close relationships with others becomes

---

2. Parley P. Pratt, *Key to the Science of Theology,* (George Q. Cannon & Sons Co.,) 1891, pp. 101–2.

magnified. Soon a great gnawing deficiency exists within himself. Though he tries with all his physical strength and endurance to satisfy this great deficiency, he will be unsuccessful. Man can feel love, closeness, caring, only through his spiritual dimension. It is only through the spiritual dimension that one feels love for others, or for self, or for God. How can we know this is so? Because those who experience and develop this spiritual dimension are the ones who "give of self" to others even when they are rejected, put down, or made fun of.

I remember as stake president receiving a call one afternoon from a Melchizedek Priesthood holder. I could tell by his voice that his business was urgent. Quickly, I reorganized my appointments for the afternoon and hurried over to the church. There this brother slowly unfolded a long tale of involvement and participation in various sexual sins — massage parlors, R- and X- rated movies, pornographic activity, masturbation. It was evident as we talked about his attitudes and feelings that he couldn't feel love within himself. He didn't feel Heavenly Father's love, nor the love of his wife and children, nor his quorum's love, though they were all there in abundance. A Church court is a cleansing process and not a condemning process, and as he progressed through this experience, through the steps of repentance, I noticed changes occurring. First, the appetites, passions, and desires of the flesh that had controlled him previously became weaker. He wanted now to do spiritual things, to help others; he wanted to do what was good and right — he wanted to stay away from those places which had tempted him previously. Next, I noticed that he began to feel the love of his wife and his children, and he was able to give them his love in return. Before, he had been depressed, alone, and frustrated. He had walked in spiritual darkness. But now he felt love, joy, and happiness; now he walked in the spiritual light. Before, he had been controlled by his physical appetites, passions, and desires; now his spiritual self was in control.

One of the inescapable results of overstimulating the desires of the flesh is a weakening of the spiritual sensitivities, creating a greater need to be loved and accepted. Those who sincerely repent and come into the spiritual light seem able to meet this need for love, but those who choose to remain in spiritual darkness inevitably try to fill their deficiency through further physical activity, and though they achieve a temporary relief of some sort, they never reach a point where they can truly love themselves or others unconditionally. They cannot achieve charity. Their minds are so centered on their own needs that they cannot give of themselves for others; therefore they cannot grow spiritually.

But as man focuses his entire being—heart, mind, and strength—on God and his realm, spiritual growth takes place, which expands his capacity for charity; he is able to feel greater love for God, for others, and for himself.

As one's spirituality increases, he is able to see events in the temporal world through spiritual eyes. Adversity has new meaning; he receives increased energy to endure. Flowers, trees, mountains, people—all contribute to increase his love for God. By his own choice, he has chosen to keep all dimensions of his being in harmony and unified.

Chapter Seven

Feeling Self-Worth

ANOTHER BARRIER TO spirituality and feeling the love of God is a feeling of low self-worth. The main source for feeling self-worth, to be valid, must be spiritual, and not simply temporal. Other sources are valid, but not central.

Definitions

1. *Spiritual worth* is the spiritual value Heavenly Father has placed upon each of his children. This worth is felt through revelation and spiritual performance.

2. *Self-worth* is the value one perceives in himself as a human being. This evaluation can include his perception of his spiritual worth, the value he puts on his performance, his physical appearance, his material possessions, his family, even his attitude toward how he feels other people value him from day to day.

3. *Feelings of self-worth* are the emotional payoffs that come through daily activities, thoughts, and experiences, measured against one's perception of his self-worth.

4. *Worldly performances* are one's acts performed in the world. The results of these acts may be negative or positive in relationship to spiritual growth. If they are done to gain the love of the world, for power, or for the honors of men, and are used as a substitute for real personal worth, then these are negative. (1 John 2:15-17.) If they are honorable and done because one is capable and wants to achieve to develop his talents, then the results will be positive.

5. *Spiritual performances* are activities done because of the love one has for Heavenly Father. These activities develop a person spiritually and build inner strength. They are done to glorify our Father in Heaven.

6. *Spiritual gifts* are free gifts to us from Heavenly Father, but we must expend effort to qualify for them. That is, we must prepare ourselves to receive them. (D&C 88:33.)

7. *Worthiness* is the measure of merit, or qualification, for spiritual gifts. As man's worthiness increases or decreases, so does his spirituality. Worthiness has nothing to do with one's basic value or spiritual worth, *but the greater one's worthiness becomes, the easier it is to feel the love of Heavenly Father.*

8. *Love* is treatment that matches our spiritual identity.[1] It is affections, and concern, expressed by warm understanding and acceptance, open approval, and appreciation; it is recognition of the great value of one's true worth, expressed inwardly as well as outwardly.

Earth life is not to prove spiritual worth

We were sent down to this earth for two main reasons: to gain a physical body, and through experience to qualify for a kingdom of glory in the next life.

How could one possibly improve his spiritual value as a son or daughter of God? If one person achieves four gold medals and

---

1. Sterling Ellsworth and Richard Ellsworth, *Getting to Know the Real You,* (Deseret Book, 1980,) p. 126.)

another achieves only one, does that increase the spiritual worth of the first person? If I succeed in teaching ten people the gospel and you succeed in teaching only one, does that mean that in the eyes of God I have greater spiritual value than you? If I sin and you do not, does that mean that God values you more than he does me? Of course not. (Ephesians 2:4–5.) Our spiritual worth was established before we were born into mortality, and nothing in our earth life will ever change it. But what we choose to do in this earth life will determine which kingdom we qualify for in the hereafter. We are here to attain worthiness, and that is based upon performance.

Who Are You?

You are a noble, faithful spirit son or daughter of God, born and reared in the courts of glory by Heavenly Parents. During the past 6,000 years, you have been taught by heavenly beings, prepared to be born upon this earth at this final time. You are unique, and Heavenly Father loves you unconditionally.

You might have been born at some other time or place, during the Dark Ages or during the flood or in Africa, Russia, Poland, or China. Why were you selected to come to the earth at this time, just before the Second Coming of Jesus Christ? Because you are qualified to do the work that needs to be done. You have talents and capabilities that are needed for this great event. You did not just happen into life at this time and place. It was *meant* for you to be here, now.

Abraham tells us:

> *Now the Lord had shown unto me, Abraham, the intelligences that were organized before the world was; and among all these there were many of the noble and great ones;*
>
> *And God saw these souls that they were good and he stood in the midst of them, and he said: These I will make my rulers; for he stood among those that were spirits, and he saw that they were good; and he said unto me: Abraham, thou art one of them; thou wast chosen before thou wast born.* (Abraham 3:22–23.)

Who are these "noble and great ones" spoken of by the Lord? Hartman Rector, Jr., in the Spokane Washington East Stake conference on January 1, 1976, said that the "noble and great ones" are the Latter-day Saints. Bruce R. McConkie in general conference, April 1974, said, "All those who receive the Melchizedek Priesthood in this life . . . were among the noble and great in that premortal sphere." Joseph Smith said, "Every man who has a calling to minister to the inhabitants of the world was ordained to that very purpose in the Grand Council of heaven before this world was."[2]

Your spirit is pure, holy, and beautiful. Brigham Young clearly stated this.

> I have taught you that the spirit is pure, when it comes into the tabernacle. The tabernacle is subject to sin, but the spirit is not. A great many think that the spirits of the children of men, when they enter the tabernacles, are totally depraved; this is a mistake. They are as holy as the angels; the devil has no power to contaminate them, he only contaminates the body.[3]

You were indeed created "a little lower than the angels" and "crowned . . . with glory and honor." (Psalm 8:5.) If you could look into the heavens and see who you really are, you would be overwhelmed with your capabilities, your talents, your spiritual qualities, and the vision of what you are able to become.

If we knew now who we really are, we would feel different about ourselves. We would be excited and enthusiastic about this life, even with its burdens and frustrations. President Lee exclaimed,

> What a difference it would make if we really sensed our divine relationship to God, our Heavenly Father, our relationship to Jesus Christ, our Savior and our elder brother, and our relationship to each other.[4]

---

2. *Teachings of the Prophet Joseph Smith*, (Deseret News Press, 1938,) p. 365.

3. Brigham Young, *Journal of Discourses*, 3:207.

4. Harold B. Lee, *Conference Report*, Oct. 1973, p. 9.

Each of us was obedient to God's laws in heaven before this world was created. We loved our Heavenly Father very much and followed his counsel. Some children in heaven were disobedient and followed Satan, but we kept our first estate in the pre-mortal existence and therefore are guaranteed one of the three degrees of glory regardless of how we live in this life, unless we qualify as a son of perdition.

> *And they who keep their first estate shall be added upon; and they who keep not their first estate shall not have glory in the same kingdom with those who keep their first estate; and they who keep their second estate shall have glory added upon their heads forever and ever. (Abraham 3:26.)*

All of us were tested and tried before we came to earth, and each of us was successful.

President Lee continues,

> Well, then, "Who am I?" Those lacking in that important understanding, and, consequently, in some degree those failing to hold themselves in the high esteem which they would have if they did understand, are lacking self-respect.
>
> ...when one does not have that love for himself... he ceases to love life. Or if he marries, he has lost his love for his wife and children—no love of home or respect for the country in which he lives, and eventually he has lost his love of God. Rebellion in the land, disorder and the lack of love in the family, children disobedient to parents, loss of contact with God, all because that person has lost all respect for himself.
>
> ...I recall the prayer of the old English weaver, "O God, help me to hold a high opinion of myself." That should be the prayer of every soul; not an abnormally developed self-esteem that becomes haughtiness, conceit, or arrogance, but a righteous, self-respect that might be

defined as "belief in one's own worth, worth to God and worth to man."[5]

Self-respect is primary to peace and happiness.

What is your value in the sight of God?

President Kimball answers this question for us:

> God is your Father. He loves you. He and your mother in heaven value you beyond any measure. They gave your eternal intelligence spirit form, just as your earthly mother and father have given you a mortal body. You are unique, one of a kind, made of the eternal intelligence which gives you claim upon eternal life.
>
> Let there be no question in your mind about your value as an individual. The whole intent of the gospel plan is to provide an opportunity for each of you to reach your fullest potential, which is eternal progression and the possibility of godhood. [6]

This summary of our eternal worth is a reminder of the privileges and responsibilities which are ours. It encourages us to value ourselves as we are valued by our eternal parents and our Elder Brother, Jesus Christ. The Savior's example and guidance from the prophets should help each of us to appreciate more fully our value and worth.[7]

Spiritual Performance

Spiritual performance occurs when one centers his heart and mind upon Heavenly Father and serves him with all his might and strength. He does home teaching, or prepares the sacrament, because he loves the Lord. He presses forward, feasting upon the words of Christ. Because he chooses to serve God out of love, great blessings are given, (D&C 130:20-21) such as the gift of

---

5. Ibid., pp. 4-5.

6. Spencer W. Kimball, *Ensign*, Nov. 1978, p. 105.

7. Relief Society Course of Study, 1980-81, Social Relations Lesson 1, p. 140.

forgiveness, the gift of the Holy Ghost, personal revelation, a celestialized body, eternal life, peace, and love. As one lives the law of tithing because of his love for Heavenly Father, blessings are given to him, (Malachi 3:8-11) but if he lives it grudgingly then his tithes are counted evil before God. (Moroni 7:8) The gift of the Holy Ghost is given to those who spiritually qualify, who keep those commandments necessary to be counted worthy of such a blessing. And so on.

An individual who thus places his heart, might, mind, and strength on Heavenly Father recognizes his own spiritual worth. He can fail in financial matters, or be rejected by others in the world, and feel the results of his own and others' negative performance, but these negative feelings will have no lasting effect upon his feelings of self-worth. He will still be able to pray and receive strength from above to sustain him. He will still strive to do well in both the spiritual and the worldly dimension because he is capable, and wants to grow, develop, and achieve.

But some persons base their feelings of self-worth in the acceptance of others. Such a person may also love Heavenly Father, but his main source of self-worth comes from others; he has a great need to be accepted by other people. Rejection by others is devastating to him. His need is so great, or becomes so great in time, that he fills it at the expense of giving love to others and growing spiritually. In time, Church work may become a burden for him because it may not meet his needs to feel loved and accepted by people.

This person eventually must turn his heart to Heavenly Father and learn to serve others because of his love of God. When he does this, he will feel love from above, and genuine love from those he serves. He will gain a true testimony of his own spiritual worth and have less need to be loved by others. He will develop a greater need to love others as his capacity to love increases.

Some persons base their feelings of self-worth upon performance in the external world. If their performance is acceptable financially, socially, or religiously, then they feel good about themselves, but if their worldly performance seems inadequate, then they feel very bad about themselves. They feel embarrassed if they do not have as much as their neighbors. They feel the Lord doesn't love them if they are not called to high positions in the Church. They feel inferior around those who have what they judge to be greater achievements. They spend much time making comparisons in order to create good or bad feelings within themselves.

The solution again is to turn to Heavenly Father to find peace in the strait and narrow path. Worldly performance should serve to help us grow and develop, but it is not an acceptable source for feelings of self-worth.

Some persons base their worth upon a rejection of any standard of performance except their own. They take refuge in saying that they don't care what others think or say. They boast, "I determine what I will do and when I want to do it." This kind of person is very self-centered; he doesn't care what his actions do to others. In reality, he is hurting inside and has a desperate need for spiritual growth, but he does not recognize that his needs are spiritual. It is easy for such a person to become involved in sin, which he will say concerns him and no one else, including his spouse, even though his spouse must suffer spiritually and perhaps physically for his decisions and actions.

This kind of person must repent and seek forgiveness from Heavenly Father so he can let the true light back into his life and establish a correct spiritual relationship with Heavenly Father.

Worldly performance is good if it is used to help a person grow and develop in good works, earning money, performing community service, exerting leadership, playing at sports, and so on. But worldly performance can be harmful if it becomes the main source for feelings of self-worth. This is because we substitute dependency upon the world for the strength of the Spirit.

The Apostle John said:

Love not the world, neither the things that are in the world. If any man love the world, the love of the Father is not in him. (I John 2:15)

Some members of the Church haven't experienced the joy of keeping the commandments solely from the love they have for Heavenly Father. Instead, they keep the commandments so they can feel acceptable as a person of worth. This kind of service is appreciated but it brings little peace or lasting happiness. In time, keeping the commandments will become a burden, not a blessing.

Unconditional Love

It is easier for one to sense his own spiritual worth as a child of God when he is experiencing unconditional love, either in giving or receiving it.

I know several members of the Church who first experience unconditional love in a Church court. They felt themselves really loved and valued, even though their sins and mistakes were openly known. These courts became the turning point in their lives, the beginning of their spiritual growth. Why? Because for the first time in their lives, they felt that there was a difference between their personal worth and their wrong (or right) acts; they felt it was really true that people could really love *them* and, at the same time, dislike what they *did*.

Some people do not feel that God loves us unconditionally. God's love for Joseph Smith, they say, is much greater than his love for a sinner. Others claim that God loves us all unconditionally, but that he loves some people more than others. President Kimball urges us all to make our love unconditional.

> But where there are special challenges, we fail only if we fail to keep trying. Let our love of each member of our family be unconditional. [8]

---

8. Spencer W. Kimball, *The Teachings of Spencer W. Kimball*, (Bookcraft, 1982,) p. 247.

He states that God's love is perfect:

> We know also that God is perfect in his love for each
> and all of us as his spirit children. When we know these
> truths, my sisters and associates in this divine cause, it
> should help us greatly as we all experience much less than
> perfect love and perfect justice in the world. If, in the
> short term, we are sometimes dealt with insensitively and
> thoughtlessly by others, by imperfect men and women, it
> may still cause us pain, but such pain and disappointment
> are not the whole of life. The ways of the world will not
> prevail, for the ways of God will triumph.[9]

Unconditional love comes from a sender to some receiver. The
receiver may or may not be willing to accept it. A parent can give
love to his teenaged son unconditionally, and the teenager may
not feel it. To feel such love from the parent (or from God), the
receiver must prepare his heart and mind to feel it. This is
according to the law of free agency. One may extend love
unconditionally, but for another to receive it, he must meet
certain conditions.

No one can force another to feel or think anything; the receiver
must decide what he will think, or feel, or do. This is why the Lord
told us that if we want to "abide" in (that is, to "feel") his love,
then we must keep his commandments. The commandments are
given to us to help us grow spiritually and, therefore, to help us
draw closer to Heavenly Father. The closer we draw to him, the
easier it is to feel his love because our capacity to feel his love has
increased.

The scriptures speak often of this kind of perfect love:

> *If ye love me, keep my commandments.* (John 14:15)

Why this charge? Because the love we feel for God will create a
desire in us to come back into his Kingdom, and the way to
accomplish that is by keeping his commandments.

---

9. Ibid., p. 244.

> *He that hath my commandments, and keepeth them, he it is that loveth me: and he that loveth me shall be loved of my Father and I will love him, and will manifest myself to him.* (John 14:21)

This may sound conditional, but it really only means that as I keep his commandments, I will be filled with his love. Why? Because I have qualified to walk in the light, where it is easier for me to feel and experience God's love.

> *If ye keep my commandments, ye shall abide in my love; even as I have kept my Father's commandments, and abide in his love.* (John 15:10)

> *If you keep not my commandments, the love of the Father shall not continue with you, therefore you shall walk in darkness.* (D&C 95:12)

It is clear that we can feel God's love if we walk in the light, and the commandments are given to show us how to walk in the light. If we choose to walk in darkness we cannot feel God's love.

When the Savior prayed for all of us before his death, he said:

> *And I have declared unto them thy name, and will declare it: that the love wherewith thou hast loved me may be in them, and I in them.* (John 17:26)

The Savior was sustained in his temporal struggles because of the love he felt from God, and now he prays that we may feel this same love from Heavenly Father.

> *But whoso keepeth his word, in him verily is the love of God perfected.* (I John 2:5)

> *He that loveth his brother abideth in the light. . . .* (I John 2:10)

> *Beloved, let us love one another: for love is of God; and every one that loveth is born of God, and knoweth God. He that loveth not knoweth not God: for God is love . . . If we love one another, God dwelleth in us, and his love is perfected in us. Hereby know we that we dwell in him, and he in us, because he hath given us of his Spirit. . . . God is love; and he that dwelleth in love dwelleth in God, and God in him.* (I John 4:7, 8, 12-13, 16)

One keeps the commandments not so God can love him more,

but so he can feel God's love more. And the more he feels the love of God for himself, the more he feels his spiritual worth. And the more one feels his worth, the more he will be able to feel this same worth for all mankind, regardless of their performance.

ASSIGNMENT

Objective: To draw closer unto Heavenly Father and grow spiritually by feeling your spiritual worth daily.

Step One:

*Come to know the truth about your spiritual
worth and value as a child of God.*

You are a noble, faithful spirit son or daughter, born and reared in the courts of glory by Heavenly Parents. Visualize where you came from. Feel the peace, the joy, and the excitement of living in the courts of glory. Feel the joy you had when you learned that you had kept your first estate and qualified to go into the second estate. Many spirits turned from God, but you were spiritually strong and had great love for your Heavenly Parents. You were one of the noble ones. You are almost equal to the angels in heaven.

Step Two:

Value yourself as God values you.

President Kimball said, "God is your Father. He loves you. He and your Mother in Heaven value you beyond any measure.... Let there be no question in your mind about your value as an individual." Performance has nothing to do with your spiritual value. You have great worth in the sight of God and in the sight of Jesus Christ. Allow these feelings of your worth to sink deeply into your mind and heart.

Step Three:

*Come to understand and feel the love
Heavenly Father has for you.*

It is perfect love, pure love, unfeigned love, unconditional love that flows from heaven. God knows you by name. He is aware of your trials, your difficulties, your struggles, and your happy moments. He loves and accepts you just the way you are right now. He wants you to improve spiritually, so you can experience greater happiness, not so he can love you more. He never stops loving you. There are no requirements on God's love for you, only requirements for you to feel his ever-flowing love.

Step Four:

*Run through your mind and heart several times
each hour how Heavenly Father loves you.*

Value yourself as God and Jesus Christ value you. President Harold B. Lee in general conference asked us to do the following:

> Now, as I come to the closing of this address, I trust that I might have given to you and others who have not yet listened to such counsel, something to stimulate some sober thinking as to who you are and from whence you came; and, in so doing, that I may have stirred up within your soul the determination to begin now to show an increased self-respect and reverence for the temple of God, your human body, wherein dwells a heavenly spirit. I would charge you to say again and again to yourselves, as the Primary organization has taught the children to sing 'I am a (son or daughter) of God' and by so doing begin today to live closer to those ideals which will make your life happier and more fruitful because of an awakened realization of who you are."[10]

Results from those who practiced
feeling their spiritual worth:

> I feel much closer to Heavenly Father. I can feel his love for me and my love for him has grown. I think he has become more real to me. He has become more a part of my

---

10. Harold B. Lee, *Conference Report*, Oct. 1973, p. 10.

everyday life. I think of him much more than I did before and I try to do what he wants. I have learned to like a couple of people I really did not care much for before.

I am praying more. I feel the love of Heavenly Father and understand the great gift he has given me. I feel I am a real daughter of God. I am happy most all the time. I don't feel afraid to meet Heavenly Father anymore.

I felt I have grown tremendously. My spiritual growth was not as it should have been and now I can feel closer to my Heavenly Father because I feel better about myself.

By loving myself, my spiritual growth has accelerated.

I feel a much more personal relationship with Heavenly Father. I realize now that he loves me unconditionally. I don't get down on myself like before. I feel like pushing on and not dwelling on my mistakes. I can overcome, the Lord and me.

I feel like a new person. I feel no one is any better than I am. I know my Heavenly Father loves me. I think differently about others and try to understand and love them.

I have a continuous need to converse with Heavenly Father. He is my strength, my light. My everyday life is a joy and so rich. Before, I felt I was not important enough to bother him with my troubles, and when I was really troubled I did not feel worthy. I feel much love, joy, and compassion towards others. And I have much love for myself, along with joy and peace. I no longer feel that God only loves others.

I have known I was a daughter of God, but now I am beginning to feel it. A neat feeling. I don't condemn myself, so I feel more joy. I show more love to others.

I understand that when I fail at something it does not affect how my Heavenly Father feels about me.

Section III

INTERACTING WITH THE SPIRITUAL DIMENSION

CONGRATULATIONS! What great progress you are making. You have accomplished step number one and are progressing on step number two.

Step No. 1

To know that you are a candidate for the celestial kingdom today and are qualified for a celestial inheritance. To have a brightness of hope that you qualify for the Savior's promises.

Step No. 2

To feel a strong desire to love God with all your heart and make these feelings dominant in all facets of your life. How do you accomplish this? You are able to develop these pure feelings of love for Heavenly Father only under the direction of the Holy Ghost.

The remaining portion of this book is designed to help you develop these feelings of love for Heavenly Father so they are so dominating; that the adversities of this life will have little control over you. For example, prayer can be used to meet the temporal pressures of life in such a way that you can maintain spiritual feelings. Or, by understanding guilt feelings correctly, you will be able to use your guilt feelings to draw closer to Heavenly Father. The intent of each gospel principle reviewed is to help you gain and maintain dominating feelings of love for your Heavenly Father. If you choose to allow the pressures of this life to become dominant over your feelings for Heavenly Father, then spiritual growth in the strait and narrow path is hindered. But if you truly love God more than all else, you will indeed remain a candidate for the celestial kingdom.

Interacting with the Spiritual Dimension

Interacting with the temporal world is an everyday event. Temporal activities like sleeping, eating, bathing, working, exercising, and talking consume nearly all the twenty-four hours in each of our days.

What does one do each day in order to interact with the spiritual dimension? Meaningful prayer, fasting for a purpose, reading scriptures for spiritual growth, being involved in healing the sick, giving priesthood blessings, helping a neighbor bury a loved one—all these would be examples of spiritual interaction.

In the past forty-eight hours, how many spiritual experiences did you have? One needs to seek to have such experiences daily; this requires planning and faith and work to achieve. These spiritual experiences are necessary in order for one to develop dominating spiritual feelings for Heavenly Father.

It is not hard for one to determine his progress in his spiritual development. All that is required is for one to evaluate how long the pressures of this temporal world are dominant. Suppose, for example, that your son got into trouble at school again. You became upset and frustrated, and wondered what you did wrong as a parent. These negative but real feelings dominated at that moment. How long did it take you to draw unto Heavenly Father until your love for him was dominant and you felt peace? How long did it take you to seek revelation and regain the influence of the Holy Ghost in your life? How long did it take you to gain the peace and spiritual calmness necessary to discipline your son in firmness and tenderness? As one grows spiritually, the time necessary to overcome these temporal feelings will increasingly shorten.

This section will review how to interact with the spiritual dimension; it will also discuss how to use the spiritual dimension to succeed in the temporal world. This is important to our growth: Many Latter-day Saints feel that since the commandments are so numerous, and time is so short, there is no way they can keep all the Lord's commandments. And, since they are not keeping all the commandments today, they feel they are not going to qualify for the celestial kingdom. Some reason there is no reason to keep trying.

It is clear that the commandments were given to help us grow spiritually. But some members of the Church use the commandments to condemn themselves and others. That is, if they are not obeying all the laws, ordinances, suggestions, and commandments given, they feel they have little worth and will never qualify for the celestial kingdom.

In chapter 10 we will review how to keep all the commandments today and enjoy it. This chapter will provide step-by-step assignments which will help us to actually experience the concepts being taught. As we come to enjoy doing the commandments, our spiritual growth will increase.

Chapter Eight

A Formula of Prayer

HOW CAN WE LEARN to love God above all else? And how can we utilize the spiritual dimension to help us both spiritually and temporally in our lives? One answer is to learn a formula of prayer.

Laman and Lemuel had problems understanding their father Lehi's dream. They were confused about the natural branches of the olive tree and also the gentiles. (1 Nephi 15:7.)

Nephi asked them, "Have you inquired of the Lord? And they said unto me: We have not, for the Lord maketh no such thing known unto us." (1 Nephi 15:8–9.)

Many people have the same problem as Laman and Lemuel. They pray but do not receive answers.

Some time ago a report came to the attention of a stake president about a father who was upset because his son was not being advanced to the Melchizedek Priesthood. The stake president made an appointment to visit this home accompanying the home teacher. Upon arriving, they felt a lack of the Spirit of God in the home; they could tell that both the father and mother were bitter about the situation.

The home teacher asked if they might kneel and have prayer. With permission from the father, everyone knelt, and the father called on the home teacher to offer the prayer. After prayer, the stake president and the home teacher reviewed the situation with the father, asking him what he felt should be done to help him and his son.

The boy had become upset several weeks before because all his friends were being advanced in the priesthood and he was not. Yet his interview with the stake president revealed that the son had a special problem which needed to be overcome before he could be ordained an elder. The stake president had outlined to the son what he was to do, and had suggested that whenever the son felt ready, he should contact the bishop. The stake president recommended that the young man become active in Young Adults, participate in missionary work, read the scriptures, and study the Institute study guide on the "Life and Teaching of Jesus."

However, rather than doing what had been suggested, the young man had rebelled because he felt embarrassed in front of his friends. He did not tell his father of his conversation with the stake president; he only said that he didn't care anymore and he felt that the stake president didn't care either.

The home teacher asked the father if he had inquired of the Lord about the situation. The father said he had been praying about it for over six weeks. "What did Heavenly Father tell you to do?" the home teacher asked.

"That is the problem," said the father, "the Lord did not tell me a thing."

"Did you follow the formula of prayer?"

The father answered, "I don't believe I know the formula of prayer."

The home teacher told him that if he would follow the formula that Jesus taught he would always receive direction from above. He would receive a burning within his bosom if the path he was on was right in the sight of Heavenly Father. If it was not right, he would feel a stupor of thought. They then asked if he was willing to try the formula, right at that moment. The father said he was willing.

"First, Brother Jones, when we talk to Heavenly Father by prayer, how does he tell us the answers to our prayers? The Lord says:

> *Yea, behold, I will tell you in your mind and in your heart by the Holy Ghost, which shall come upon you and which shall dwell in your heart.*
>
> *Now behold, this is the spirit of revelation.* (D&C 8:2-3.)

"You see, as we turn our minds and hearts to God, we will have thoughts placed in our minds. How will we know if these thoughts are from God? Because we will feel in our hearts that these thoughts are good."

"But can't I have good thoughts on my own? How do I know if these thoughts are mine or from heaven?" inquired Brother Jones.

"Good question. Let us review a few principles."

Principle No. One

God will reveal his answers to you
in your mind and heart.

"That is why he says, 'For as he thinketh in his heart, so is he.' (Proverbs 23:7.) We tend to do those things that make us feel good. Remember, Satan reveals thoughts in the mind and confirms in the stomach. Whenever you have had negative thoughts about yourself, you will feel those pains in the stomach. You feel rotten about yourself, worthless.

If we learn to follow God's way, we can see clearly our faults and still feel good about ourselves. It makes little difference whether the thought came from your own mind or from Heavenly Father's. The key is whether the Holy Ghost confirms the thought as being righteous and valid. If the thought comes from your mind and the Holy Ghost confirms it as being valid, then you are to be congratulated. Your mind is being inspired to receive answers from your past experience and the experiences of others, as well as from heaven."

Principle No. Two

We are told by the prophets that
one can know good from evil with
a perfect knowledge. (Moroni 7:15-18.)

"We do not need to doubt these good thoughts and feelings, for if they are good they come from Him. Moroni says that we can know good from evil as clearly as we can tell daylight from darkness."

Principle No. Three

We cannot receive answers to our prayers
if we allow doubt to remain in our minds.

"In order to receive revelation we must condition our minds. We must believe that we shall receive revelation from heaven when requested:

> *Or what man is there of you, whom if his son asks bread, will he give him a stone? Or if he asks a fish, will he give him a serpent? If ye then, being evil, know how to give good gifts unto your children, how much more shall your Father which is in heaven give good things to them that ask Him?* (Matthew 7:9-11)

> *If any of you lack wisdom, let him ask of God, that giveth to all men liberally, and upbraideth not, and it shall be given him.*
> *But let him ask in faith, nothing wavering. . . .* (James 1:5-6)

> *. . . if you do not cast it out by your unbelief, that ye will resist the Spirit of the Lord. . . .* (Alma 32:28)

> *Remember that without faith you can do nothing, therefore, ask in faith. . . .* (D&C 8:10)

"Joseph Smith taught as reported in the *Lectures on Faith* that 'doubt and faith do not exist in the same person at the same time.' As we exercise our faith that God is directing us, through our faith he can and will lead us."

Principle No. Four

As we use this formula of prayer as found in Matthew 7:7, we will come to know that the revelations are from him and that which we receive is right.

Ask and it shall be given you; seek and ye shall find; knock and it shall be opened unto you. (Matt. 7:7)

"This formula is: 'Ask, Seek, Knock,' not merely 'Ask.' It is perpendicular, so:

A
S
K

"This formula of prayer, which was taught by the Savior, gives us the way to receive revelation:

A—'For everyone that asketh receiveth.'

"As we petition Heavenly Father, we must make it clear what we desire. (Remember that he will not do for us those things we can do for ourselves.) We need Heavenly Father's help and support as we overcome earthly weaknesses. For example, one may desire to become a better person. He should ask God to give him ideas on what he can do to become a better person; God will help him and give him strength.

S—'And he that seeketh findeth.'

"Find what? As we seek, we will find the way to accomplish the things we asked about in our prayer. For instance, one may have asked God to help him become a better husband. He must now allow God to place the ways in his mind to accomplish this. Heavenly Father might place in his mind the following suggestions:

1. Take wife out once a week.

2. Say thank you for each meal.

3. Help her when she is tired.

4. Relieve her of the children from time to time.

5. Pay attention when she talks about her day.

6. Express real feelings when you talk together (negative or positive).

7. Look for the good she does and express your appreciation.

8. Give her some free time to spend as she would like.

K—'And to him that knocketh it shall be opened.'

"What does it mean to knock? It means *to do*. That is, we must carry out the ideas that Heavenly Father suggests. Remember that one still is calling on Heavenly Father under prayer as he carries out this phase. As we do, we will come to know what we are doing is not only good, but is fulfilling the request in our prayer. The burning we will feel inside confirms our actions. Now, Brother Jones, do you understand the formula of prayer?"

Brother Jones replied that he did and was ready to use it in behalf of his son. Everyone knelt, and the father prayed:

(Ask)

"Our Father which is in heaven, we kneel before thee this hour with complete dependence upon thy Spirit. We are grateful for thee and feel thy love and concern for us. May we be prepared to receive revelation from thee now concerning my son. Thou knowest his desires and difficulties in preparing for the Melchizedek Priesthood. We desire to help him. Please reveal to us what we can do to assist him in this preparation. We pray in the name of Jesus Christ. Amen."

(Seek)

All arose and the home teacher suggested that the father take a blank sheet of paper and write the problem down as he understood it. Next, he suggested that the father open his mind and heart to Heavenly Father, and in that framework write on the paper whatever came into his mind. The father did so, and wrote the following:

> I want to help my son get the desire to prepare himself for the Melchizedek Priesthood.

> Ask the stake president what I can do to help.

> Ask the bishop what I can do to help.

> Do more things with my son. Get closer to his feelings.

> Pray more and feel after the Holy Ghost.

(Knock)

The father then asked the stake president what he could do, and the stake president reviewed, except for confidential matters, what had taken place in his interview with the young man. The father now understood for the first time the suggested areas the son had been asked to work on.

The next Sunday, the father met with the bishop of the ward and asked him how he might help his son. The bishop reviewed the problem as he saw it; he told him the suggestions he had given the young man. Among these recommendations was that the young man request a blessing from his father.

The father and mother talked things through seriously and honestly. They got their lives back in order and then talked openly with their son about all that had transpired. The father gave his son a blessing. Later, both father and son spent much time together in the scriptures and doing special things together. The son would still become moody and close up at various times, but the father followed the formula of prayer again and again to help his son. In the following three-month period, the father grew as much as the son did.

And the father did receive a burning within his bosom as he carried out the process of prayer. Of course, there were times when he did not feel anything particularly spiritual. But he refused to allow doubt to hinder progress. He pressed forward, for he knew that what he was doing was good and right.

Sometimes his son did not want his help, but the father continued to show love and concern. Three months later, the young man received the Melchizedek Priesthood. Later, he went on a mission.

This prayer formula is a step-by-step procedure which can provide spiritual help with our temporal problems also. It can be used in every area, in building an estate, improving a marriage, solving family problems, or improving skills for employment. To succeed temporally takes great effort, and sometimes our efforts fall short of the mark. But Heavenly Father will step in and make up the difference if we follow his direction. But we must remember that his perspective of our situation is larger than ours is. Sometimes he may not guide us as we desire to be guided. But always our spiritual growth will be increased, and there will be no setback to our salvation.

Note that the title of this chapter is **A** Formula of Prayer and not **the** Formula of Prayer. We do not mean to suggest that there is only one way to approach deity. However, should we be having difficulty receiving spiritual help in either spiritual or temporal affairs, this approach certainly may help. The next chapter provides answers to questions which may arise in applying a formula of prayer.

Chapter Nine

Questions and Answers
On the Formula of Prayer

"I HATE TO BOTHER Heaveny Father about all my problems."

Many people feel unworthy of spiritual help and therefore do not want to bother Heavenly Father, especially on their little problems. These thoughts are contrary to what the Savior taught:

> *Look unto me in every thought; doubt not, fear not.* (D&C 6:36)

> *For if ye would hearken unto the Spirit which teacheth a man to pray ye would know that ye must pray; for the evil spirit teacheth not a man to pray, but teacheth him that he must not pray.*

> *But behold, I say unto you that ye must pray always, and not faint; that ye must not perform any thing unto the Lord save in the first place ye shall pray unto the Father in the name of Christ, that he will consecrate thy performance unto thee, that thy performance may be for the welfare of thy soul.* (2 Nephi 32:8-9.)

> *Yea, and cry unto God for all thy support; yea, let all thy doings be unto the Lord, and whithersoever thou goest let it be in the Lord; yea, let*

all thy thoughts be directed unto the Lord; yea, let the affections of thy heart be placed upon the Lord forever.

Counsel with the Lord in all thy doings, and he will direct thee for good. (Alma 37:36-37.)

"But, aren't we supposed to do things on our own?"

If one is seeking to become dependent upon heaven before one makes a move, then he will never become like God. We know that man is equipped to make decisions and to act on his own. (Helaman 14:30.) Why then run back to Heavenly Father every time one needs to make a decision?

Everyone who has ever lived was placed upon this earth to walk alone through many experiences — physical, mental, financial, marital—with accidents, death, warfare, loss of loved ones, business and social success and failure, and so on. Heavenly Father will not go through these experiences for us. But he is available to guide us and strengthen us as we walk through these growth experiences. We should stay close to him for guidance and advice. His advice is free, and it is always correct. Heavenly Father is the best partner possible if we intend to be successful. As the saying goes, "You can live without God, but you cannot succeed without him."

But often we ask for help and receive none. When the path we are on is right, Heavenly Father chooses to let us walk alone. We must plan, challenge ourselves, endure, and exercise faith to overcome, and the heavens can and will give assistance and direction. If Heavenly Father feels his help is needed, he will intervene in our behalf. By checking with heaven in all things as we perform to the best of our abilities, we can become prepared to receive revelation when it is needed. Bruce R. McConkie has said:

> And so we're faced with two propositions. One is that we ought to be guided by the spirit of inspiration, the spirit of revelation. The other is that we're here under a direction to use our agency, to determine what we ought to do on our own; and we need to strike a fine balance

between these two, if we're going to pursue a course that will give us joy, satisfaction, and peace in this life and lead to eternal reward in our Father's kingdom. [1]

The solution is to always keep the channels to heaven open for guidance. No one will receive revelation until he exercises his free agency and decides what he should do to solve each problem. (D&C 9:7-9.) Heavenly Father is always there to help when help is necessary; when we use the formula of prayer, we can be assured that the solution, or the enduring, or the overcoming, will be achieved.

Elder George Q. Cannon testifies:

> We of all people should be happy and joyful. When the clouds seem the darkest and most threatening and as though the storm is ready to burst upon us with all its fury, we should remain calm, serene, and undisturbed, for if we have the faith we profess to have, we know that God is in the storm, in the cloud, or in the threatened danger, and that he will not let it come upon us only as far as it is necessary for our good and for our salvation. [2]

"Does Heavenly Father always hear my prayers?"

Yes. (Alma 18:32; Matthew 6:8.)

"What preparations do I need to make in order to receive revelation?"

1. You must attain a state of mind known as faith, by which, nothing wavering (James 1:5-7), you can remove all doubts and fears. (D&C 6:36; Alma 32:8.)
2. You must have love for God and all men. (2 Nephi 31:20; Matthew 5:22-24.)
3. You must qualify for the companionship of the Holy Ghost. (D&C 8:2-3.)

President Marion G. Romney has stated:

---

1. Bruce R. McConkie, "Agency or Inspiration?" *New Era,* Jan. 1975, pp. 38-39.
2. George Q. Cannon, *Journal of Discourses,* 15:375.

If you would obtain and keep the guidance of the Spirit, you can do it by following this simple three-part program:

First: Pray diligently. Learn to talk to the Lord. Call upon His name in great faith and confidence.

Second: Live righteously. Repent of your sins by confessing them and forsaking them. Then conform to the teachings of the gospel and give service to the church.

Third: Study. Study the gospel as you might sciences and other scholastic courses.

If you will do these things, you will get the guidance of the Holy Spirit, and you will go through this world successfully regardless of what the people of this world do. [3]

Use the above as a checklist to see if you are prepared to receive revelation. If not, then you must prepare yourself so that you may enjoy that gift.

"Why do I feel confused many times when I pray?"

There could be several reasons. Perhaps you are not living worthy of the companionship of the Holy Ghost. Or perhaps you really do not want to hear the answer that you know is right. Perhaps you have not made the spiritual preparations necessary to receive an answer. Perhaps you are trying to receive answers when you do not like yourself or someone else.

For example, Tom is trying to decide between going to church today or staying home because he has a headache. As long as Tom keeps asking Heavenly Father which one he should do, he will only maintain confusion. Why? Because the laws of heaven require that he decide himself what to do, and then ask for a confirmation. (D&C 9:8-9.)

Marion G. Romney suggests:

Study your problems, and prayerfully make a decision.

---

3. Marion G. Romney, "How to Improve My Communications with the Lord," *Improvement Era*, April 1966, p. 275.

Then take that decision and say to the Lord, in simple, honest supplication, "Father, I want to make the right decision. I want to do the right thing. This is what I think I should do; let me know if it is the right course." Doing this, you can get the burning in your bosom, if your decision is right. If you do not get the burning, then change your decision and submit a new one. [4]

Therefore, in our example, Tom finally decides to go to church, and as he is making preparations to go, his heart is still drawn out in prayer; (Alma 34:27.) he will thus receive a good feeling in his heart, and know that he will be blessed for going.

Or, Tom could decide to stay home and rest so that his headache can go away. As his heart is drawn out in prayer as he rests, he will either receive a good feeling or he will receive feelings that he is denying himself certain blessings in choosing to not attend church.

If one is trying to decide between two investments, he should select one and then ask, seek, and knock. During those three phases, he will receive a good feeling or a negative feeling. Remember that each person is responsible for his own choice and for the results of that choice. If the investment comes out sour, he ought to be careful in concluding that prayer is of little worth, for that loss may be the very training that he will need for the next investment analysis, which could prove fruitful and through which he may recover any previous losses. He should remember that it may take several losses before he is trained to select investments that will help him reach his goal of financial independence.

"What happens if I am trying to decide between several investments and I have not yet made up my mind? How can the Lord help me?"

If I had not yet decided on an investment, but felt a need to

---

4. Ibid., p. 275.

explore more before deciding, I would use the formula of prayer to accomplish this exploration. For example, my family decided to look at the possibility of going into a family business. We thought we might open a bookstore because the boys could work there during the regular high school year, and the girls during the summer months, to earn money for college. As we prayed about it as a family, we all felt good about the project. This was our confirmation from Heavenly Father that He felt pleased. We knew, however, that even though Heavenly Father felt good about it, this did not mean that the business would succeed. We still had to do the work, learn the business, pay the costs and accomplish our objectives.

Next, we entered the *seeking phase.* Ideas, suggestions, and problems were placed on the blackboard: finances, building site, how much time would the project take, how would the economy affect it all? Assignments were made to seek out the necessary solutions and answers.

The *knocking phase* was now in operation. As we gathered our facts, ideas came into our minds of other things we should look for, such as competition, the best location of the store, and the time and devotion the store would demand. In this we again sought for Heavenly Father's help. When at last all the facts were in, we felt excited about the available possibilities. But were we willing to lock ourselves into a business which would not allow us the flexibility to go and come as we desired; this became very important. Flexibility has always been an important factor in our lives. After much consideration and further prayer we knew that the price we would have to pay to enter the bookstore business was too great.

Our family experiences show that we need to select and evaluate before asking for confirmation. We need to carefully evaluate the price so that we can make a commitment. When we are able to make a commitment to act, then we can expect the confirmation. Some people merely ask, and when they receive a warm feeling inside as a confirmation, they assume that this means that the Lord will make sure of their financial success; in actuality, it means only that the Lord approved of their coming experience. Having not really evaluated the price they will have to pay for the experience, and faced at last with paying that price, they begin to question the Lord and the value of prayer. Or, worse yet, when the price proves too great and they fail, or really have to struggle to pay the price, they assume that having had a confirmation they must have failed the Lord, because if they were more worthy the venture would have succeeded.

"I have felt good during my prayers, but what I have prayed about still did not come out as I expected."

Some members make the mistake of assuming that Heavenly Father has approved their whole package when they receive a good feeling in the asking phase. But the confirmation is simply the signal to continue in the formula of prayer — to study it out and thoroughly evaluate the price. My wife and I prayed about going into a business venture and we felt good about it. Once we got all the facts, we then had to decide whether the venture was good and honorable, and whether we wanted to pay the price. We did decide to pay the price and then asked for a further confirmation of that decision, and received confirmation. But five years later we were broke and heavily in debt. Did this mean that Heavenly Father had deserted us, or that we were unworthy, or that our experience was of little value? Not at all. We found that in the process of working toward our prayed-for level of financial independence, our business failures were the very training we needed to at last succeed.

I know a family that twice went broke as they sought their goal of financial independence. Because they were honest in their business dealings, they tightened their belts and found ways to double their income in order to pay their debts. When the debts were paid off, they had increased their ability to earn money and now could invest the extra money earned. They later suffered another business failure and had to find ways to again double their income. The interesting thing is that fifteen years before, they had set a goal to be financially independent in twenty years and Heavenly Father had approved. At the end of the twentieth year they achieved their goal.

In the above example, it took the couple fifteen years to prepare themselves to understand and accept the plans needed to reach their goal. After the plan was received and finally understood, it took only five years for them to achieve the goal. This principle is true in all of our relationships. It is as true in improving a marriage, or family situations, as it is in improving a business.

"What is the difference between confirmation, stupor of thought, and no answer?"

First of all, each of us has the light of Christ and really can tell with a perfect knowledge the difference between good and evil.

Secondly, assuming we are using the light that we have been given, we will receive the answer to our prayer in our mind and in our heart. (D&C 8:2-3.) We will feel a warm sensation within our breast. (D&C 9:8.) If we are seeking more light and knowledge, or ideas to answer our prayers (in the seeking phase), we will experience a flow of intelligence in our minds which will lead us toward what we needed to answer our prayer.[5] We will experience the three signs of this type of revelation: it will enlighten our understanding, enlarge our soul, and be very delicious to us. We will feel a desire for more of this type of help. (Alma 32:28.)

"But what happens if we receive no answer?"

First, we should check to see if our request is appropriate. (James 4:3.)

Second, we should evaluate whether our faith is sufficient to expect an answer and to abide by the answer when it is received.

---

5. *Teachings of the Prophet Joseph Smith,* p. 151.

Do we feel good about ourselves, Heavenly Father, and others?

Third, have we followed the formula of prayer—made a decision, sought for help, then done all we could do?

Finally, if time is short, and we have done all things to receive revelation, then Heavenly Father is allowing us to act on our own.

Elder Richard Scott of the First Quorum of Seventy, has suggested three possible results of right prayer:

> Permit me to share something with you that I feel is sacred. I have found by personal experience, and have had confirmed so repeatedly that I know it is true, that when we follow the laws of prayer given us of God one of three things happens. First, we will feel that peace, that comfort, that assurance, that certainty, that our decision is right; or second, we will feel that uncomfortableness, that stupor of thought, and we know that what we have chosen is wrong; or third—and this is the difficult one— we feel nothing. What do you do when you do not feel an answer? I have come to thank the Lord with all my heart when that occurs, for it is an evidence of his trust.[6]

President Joseph F. Smith said:

> The presentation or "gift" of the Holy Ghost simply confers upon a man the right to receive at any time, when he is worthy of it and desires it, the power and light of truth of the Holy Ghost, although he may often be left to his own spirit and judgment.[7]

Sometimes Heavenly Father may not care which activity we engage in, for both may be good, both may bring us needed growth and experience. It is by design that he allows us to decide and act. (D&C 58:26-28.) We can choose several places to live and

---

6. Richard G. Scott, *1978 Devotional Speeches of the Year,* (Provo: Brigham Young University Press, 1979,) p. 102.

7. Joseph F. Smith, *Gospel Doctrine,* 9th ed., (Salt Lake City: Deseret Book Co., 1952,) pp. 60-61.

several different occupations to earn a living—all of which may be acceptable to him. But we still need to check with him to see if our decision *does* matter, or if we need to seek more ways to determine the price we will have to pay to accomplish the purposes of our prayer. If we have time, we may follow President Romney's suggestion:

> I know from my own experience that prayer is the pathway by which we may come into contact with God and receive direction from Him. There have been times in my life when it was very difficult for me to get through to the Lord and when I've had to fast and pray for periods each week over long months of time. But it can be done, and you can pray to the Father and receive help in your problems. One need not make serious mistakes in life. If you can learn to walk by the Spirit, you can make every decision in your life correctly. [8]

"How do I know if the Holy Ghost is speaking to me or not?"

Do what you feel impressed to do, and you will know. (John 8:32; D&C 84:46.) Most often, we walk by faith. We do not have a perfect knowledge. (Alma 32:21.) We must walk to the edge of the light and then into the darkness where we have little or no experience, and act with faith. [9]

Try this: Write in your journal what you have felt impressed to do, and then do it. Then several months later go back and review your journal. You will find that with some modifications, your prayer was answered.

Those who ask "How do I know?" usually are not following the revelations already received. They choose to doubt the revelation because they are not sure that it will work. They are not willing to

---

8. Marion G. Romney, "How to Improve My Communication with the Lord," *Improvement Era*, April 1966, p. 275.

9. Boyd K. Paker "Faith," *Improvement Era*, Nov. 1968, p.62.

walk by faith, and choose to remove all doubts and uncertainty from their minds, and just trust Heavenly Father.

For most people, the confirmation of the Spirit comes more often in the "knocking" phase than in the "asking" phase. But many people never move beyond the "asking" phase, and therefore they seldom experience the burning within their bosom.

It has been my experience that one must keep his mind and heart open to Heavenly Father during all phases of prayer. As one carries out the "to do" list in the "knocking" phase, and as one has the true attitude of prayer, more revelation comes. The list of possibilities is expanded. We must then ask Heavenly Father for additional help or insight to carry out the suggestions received in the "seeking" phase.

"When I receive a good feeling about my request, does this mean that Heavenly Father has approved the whole package?"

A young man wanted to get married. He was dating several girls. He was praying one evening about marrying a specific young lady whom he really liked. A warm "yes" came over his whole being. He arose happily from his knees because he knew he had received a confirmation.

Did Heavenly Father say yes to his getting married, and that he would surely be very happy with this young lady? Did Heavenly Father also say the young man was ready for marriage, financially and spiritually? And that the young lady would marry him? And that next month was the time to get married? The results of one's actions are always his own responsibility. Receiving answers to prayer does not transfer his responsibility to Heavenly Father.

If we go back to the formula of prayer, we can see that this young man was only in the "asking" phase. When he got a confirmation he now needed to go to step number two, "seek."

He should ask, "What can I do next to prepare for marriage?" Inspiration would flow to him, and as he carried out these suggestions, he would learn more about the prices of his prospective marriage. Perhaps he would begin to see some areas where he needed more time to prepare.

At the same time, the young lady would need to do her own praying and listening and selecting. As they both worked through the formula they would know if and when they should be married; and when they had made their decision, they would be ready to ask Heavenly Father to confirm their decision.

Regardless of the difficulties these two people would surely experience in marriage, they would always know that Heavenly Father had said "yes" and that they could make it together, if they so chose. They would need to accept full responsibility for their decisions and be willing to struggle and sacrifice in their marriage so that they might have their prayers fulfilled as Heavenly Father had promised.

"Do we always feel the influence of the Holy Ghost if we are worthy?"

No. Read Hugh B. Brown's statement as reported by Truman Madsen, then a mission president in New England:

> It was at the Mission Home. We sat down in the midst of a tight schedule with President Hugh B. Brown. Several missionaries, luxuriating in his spirit, grasped at the moment to ask questions.
>
> "Can you have the Spirit of God all the time?" asked one. "And how do you cope with the dark hours?"
>
> He looked away for a moment, reflecting.
>
> "My life experience proves to me one thing. The Lord knows. And the Lord cares.
>
> "When you are blessed with the communion or the 'sunshine' of the Spirit, you bask in it, drink it in, to prepare for the hours when you are left to yourself; to pull you through the darkness.

"I have never been able to synchronize my watch with the Lord's timetable. We are His instruments and His will does not always correspond with ours. But we must go on. Or we are lost and have no promise.

"Even the Savior cried out on the cross, 'Why hast Thou forsaken me?'"[10]

The Holy Ghost withdraws itself from time to time in order for us to become like God. We need to have the experience of walking according to our own light and knowledge. We must pray, read the scriptures, love God and others, and then choose what we will do to succeed. We are responsible. Heavenly Father wants us to succeed, but we must go through the experience ourselves.

Even the Savior in his final hour had to suffer for the sins of the world without the help of the Spirit. He had to walk that alone. But he knew that the course he was on was correct. He had strong confirmation of that. But he still requested that the cup might pass, but nevertheless "thy will be done."

---

10. Truman G. Madsen, "Can You Have the Spirit of God All the Time?" *Church News*, (Deseret News, Salt Lake City, Feb. 29, 1964,) p. 5.

Chapter Ten

Goals and Sanctification
(How to Keep All the Commandments)

ONE THING THAT WILL help us function in the spiritual dimension is to keep the commandments. As we do, we will enjoy a greater portion of the gift of the Holy Ghost. How can it be done? Let's begin with a few basic principles.

Doctrine of Justification

How do you know that what you do is acceptable to heaven? In a Melchizedek Priesthood Study Guide we were instructed as follows:

> What then is the law of justification? It is simply this: "All covenants, contracts, bonds, obligations, oaths, vows, performances, connections, associations, or expectations" (D&C 132:7), in which men must abide to be saved and exalted, must be entered into and performed in righteousness so that the Holy Spirit can *justify the candidate* for salvation in what has been done ... an act that if justified by the Spirit is one that is sealed by the Holy Spirit of Promise, or in other words, ratified and approved

by the Holy Ghost. This law of justification is the provision the Lord has placed in the gospel to assure that no unrighteous performance will be binding on earth and in heaven, and that no person will add to his position or glory in the hereafter by gaining an unearned blessing.

We know when something is justified because the Spirit will be with us. (Moses 6:60.) The companionship of the Spirit, graciously extended by the Lord, is the witness or evidence of justification.

If a person sincerely repents of past mistakes, the Spirit may return and again justify the actions of that man, thus assuring that they are acceptable to God. [1]

Elder McConkie has explained how justification becomes operative:

As with all other doctrines of salvation, justification is available because of the atoning sacrifice of Christ, but it becomes operative in the life of an individual only on conditions of personal righteousness. [2]

When it comes time to inherit the gift of the celestial kingdom, we will not give the Savior a list of all our deeds and ask, "Where do I pick out my forty acres?" Our deeds will never equal an inheritance in the celestial kingdom. But Heavenly Father will give us the gift of entrance into his kingdom as long as we qualify for that gift. As long as we fulfill the demands of justice we can receive the gift. On what basis can we be assured that what we are doing will be acceptable to our Heavenly Father? By our having the companionship of the Holy Ghost and doing things in this life for Heavenly Father, then we can know that our works are acceptable.

When we qualify, we are *justified* to come back into the presence

---

1. *Melchizedek Priesthood Personal Study Guide,* 1978–79, (The Church of Jesus Christ of Latter-day Saints, Salt Lake City, 1978,) p. 46.

2. Bruce R. McConkie, *Mormon Doctrine,* p. 408.

of God, even though we have sinned, because of the sacrifice of the Savior and our righteous works.

Doctrine of Sanctification

How does one eventually overcome the effects of sin? By the law of sanctification. As one walks in the strait and narrow path, daily feeling the influence of the Holy Ghost, his spiritual self will grow and expand. As he continues in the path, loving God and all men, he will reach the point where his strongest desire is to serve Heavenly Father. (D&C 88:67-68; 2 Nephi 31:20.) His past sins will no longer have any *negative effects* upon him. If any mistakes in the past are recalled, they will be felt simply as experiences to learn from. He will have no negative feelings of self-worth — he has overcome.

The 1978-1979 Melchizedek Priesthood Study Guide reviews sanctification:

> I will put my own definition to the term sanctification, and say it consists in overcoming every sin and bringing all into subjection to the laws of Christ. **God has placed in us a pure spirit; when this reigns predominant, without let or hindrance, and triumphs over the flesh and rules and governs and controls as the Lord controls the heavens and the earth, this I call the blessing of sanctification.**

> Sanctification cannot be achieved by man alone; it requires the powers of heaven together with his sincere labors and desires. (Also Alma 41:3, and D&C 20:31, 32.)[3]

Model of Mind and Heart

According to the scriptures there are several functions of the mind and heart. On the next page is a model which can be used to help us understand their functions in overcoming the world. Following the diagram, several scriptures are listed referring to each dimension.

---

3. *Melchizedek Priesthood Personal Study Guide,* 1978-79, p. 47.

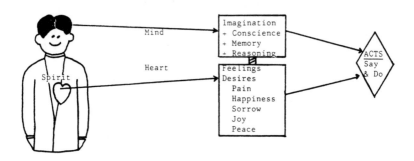

Spirit

And thus he was baptized, and the Spirit of God descended upon him, and thus he was born of the Spirit, and become quickened in the inner man. (Moses 6:65)

For as the body without the spirit is dead . . . (James 2:26)

The veil shall be rent and you shall see me and know that I am — not with the carnal neither natural mind, but with the spiritual. (D&C 67:10)

Imagination

And God saw that the wickedness of man was great in the earth, and that every imagination of the thought of his heart was only evil. (Genesis 6:5)

Do you look forward with an eye of faith, and view this mortal body raised in immortality, and thus corruption raised in incorruption, to stand before God to be judged according to the deeds which have been done in the mortal body?

I say unto you, can you **imagine to yourselves** *that ye* **hear the voice of the Lord, saying** *unto you, in that day: come unto me ye* *blessed, for behold, your works have been the works of righteousness upon the face of the earth?* (Alma 5:15, 16)

And thou, Solomon my son, know thou the God of thy father, and serve him with a perfect heart and with a willing mind: for the Lord searcheth all hearts, and understandeth all the imaginations of the thoughts: if thou seek him, he will be found of thee. (I Chronicles 28:9)

Conscience

For God doth know that in the day ye eat thereof, then your eyes shall be opened, and ye shall be as gods, knowing good and evil. (Genesis 3:5)

He that is without sin among you, let him first cast a stone at her ... and they which heardst, being convicted by their own conscience, went out one by one. (John 8:7, 9)

Apostle Paul said, "I have lived in all good conscience before God." (Acts 23:1)

... charity out of a pure heart, and of a good conscience, and of faith unfeigned. (I Timothy 1:5)

Yea, and I know that good and evil have come before all men; he that knoweth not good from evil is blameless; but he that knoweth good and evil, to him it is given according to his desires, whether he desireth good or evil, life or death, joy or remorse of conscience. (Alma 28:5)

Memory

I was harrowed up by the memory of my many sins, behold I remembered also to have heard my Father prophesy unto the people concerning the coming of one Jesus Christ....

Now as my mind caught hold of this thought, I cried within my heart....

And now, behold, when I thought this, I could remember my pains no more, yea, I was harrowed up by the memory of my sins no more. (Alma 36:17–19)

Remember not the sins of my youth, nor my transgressions. (Psalms 25:7)

Sacrament Prayer—"... *do this in remembrance of me.*"

Reasoning

And now come, saith the Lord, . . . let us reason together, that ye may understand. (D&C 50:10)

And immediately when Jesus perceived in his spirit that they so reasoned within themselves, he said unto them, why reason ye these things in your heart? (Mark 2:8)

The Lord sent forth the fulness of his gospel, his everlasting covenant, reasoning in plainness and simplicity — to prepare the weak for those things which are coming on the earth. (D&C 133:57, 58)

Heart

As he thinketh in his heart so is he. (Proverbs 23:7)

. . . have removed their hearts far from me. (Matthew 15:8)

Turn the hearts of the fathers to the children. (Malachi 4:6)

Blessed are the pure in heart. (Matthew 5:8)

Committed adultery with her already in his heart. (Matthew 5:28)

Where your treasure is, there will be your heart also. (Matthew 6:21)

I am meek and lowly in heart. (Matthew 11:27)

Out of the heart proceedeth evil thoughts. (Matthew 15:19)

Out of the abundance of the heart his mouth speaketh. (Luke 6:45)

God knoweth your heart. (Luke 16:15)

Desires

. . . fulfilling the desires of the flesh. (Ephesians 2:3)

. . . began to feel a desire for the welfare of my brethren. (Enos 1:9)

. . . granteth unto men according to their desires. (Alma 29:4)

. . . according to the desires of their hearts. (D&C 137:9)

Focus on Future, Past, or Present

How can this model help us? It appears that one can focus his mind on the things of the future, the past, or the present. For example, one can walk along the road and see the scenery or stop a friend and talk or participate in sports, all of which is in the present moment. He can use his conscience to determine if what he is doing is good or evil. He can use his memory to recall things to talk about or help him in his sports. His reasoning faculty is used to look at the pros and cons of each decision, weighing the possible results of each choice.

In this process, the imagination is a powerful tool. The imagination is used to gain knowledge, to develop faith and hope, to draw close to spiritual matters. Moroni suggests what one should hope for — he says, "and what is it that ye shall hope for? Behold I say unto you that ye shall have hope through the atonement of Christ and the power of his resurrection, to be raised unto life eternal." (Moroni 7:41) One needs to picture in his mind, and feel in his heart, his being raised up unto eternal life. He needs to spend some of his present moments developing faith in Jesus Christ.

How is this done? By picturing the Savior in one's imagination and feeling after him. While reading the scriptures one can see Christ's travels, feel his suffering, understand his counsels, and feel his expressions of love. Through this mental experience, one can learn truths that can be used in dealing with the realities of life.

For example, if one is being put down by someone else, what are his options? He can *believe* what is being said about him and feel in his heart rejection, worthlessness, stupid, dumb, and lose hope, faith, and charity. Or he can open his imagination and ask, "What would Christ do in this situation? What would He do to help this person overcome *his* problem?" If this individual has a witness of his own spiritual worth in the sight of God, a hope in *his* personal resurrection and eternal life, and a love of God and all men, what will be the results when *he sees and feels after the Savior?* He will feel love, joy, and peace in this situation of persecution and will have great inner strength. He will be able to feel love for the person who is putting him down. He will be sensitive to the feelings of this person and pray for him. (Matthew 5:43, 44.)

If one has developed an inner strength that comes from a testimony of one's spiritual worth, hope in Christ, and a daily personal relationship with Heavenly Father and Jesus Christ, then he is prepared to overcome the adversities of this life. This person can lose everything like money, recognition, loved ones, and still overcome the sorrow and pain. How? Because his strength comes from above. He can open his imagination and heart unto God and receive strength. (2 Nephi 22:2; Alma 26:12.) As one reads the scriptures and ponders them in his heart his imagination will see and his heart will feel the words of the Savior. He will feel his love, his desire to save all men, and come to know of the purpose of this life. The scriptures will become alive and delicious to him; his soul will be enlightened. (Alma 32:28) Will this spiritual experience be real? Yes, according to Alma. (Alma 32:35.)

I personally believe that this inner spiritual direction will help us over the adversities of this life in relationship to our dominating feelings. For example, if someone is finding fault with me, I will experience certain feelings, and if I pray unto Heavenly Father and the feelings I have for him are deeper and stronger than the current negative feelings, I will be able to control these negative feelings and soon God's love can fill my being as I continue to feel after Heavenly Father.

The Emotions Follow the Mind

It appears that man can only think deeply about one thing at a time. (James 1:8) And as a man thinketh, his emotions seem to follow. If a person thinks about a lovely lake, feels the sunlight, hears the birds singing, his body will relax and he can feel peace and at ease. *The emotions respond to what he holds in the mind.* As a person holds negative thoughts of the past in his mind (mistakes, sins, criticism by others, embarrassing situations) soon he will feel corresponding feelings. As one thinks of being wealthy, or poor, accepted, or rejected, the emotions are present. When one drives down the street, he can choose to notice the for-sale signs, etc. *Even though he has the right to change his thoughts to other things,* if the emotional pull of buying a home is greater than anything else, at the moment, his mind will remain on the possible dream of buying a home. Anything in the environment that relates to buying a home will come to his attention. It takes great effort to change one's mind to things that don't have the same emotional pull. If two or three thoughts pass through the mind, the one with the greatest emotions attached to it will be brought back to take center stage.

Free to Choose and to Act

Each person is free to choose what he will hold in his mind and therefore what he will believe and feel in his heart. Heavenly Father told Adam and Eve that they were free to choose.

> *But of the tree of the knowledge of good and evil, thou shalt not eat of it, nevertheless, thou mayest choose for thyself, for it is given unto thee;....* (Moses 3:17)

The Savior told Joseph Smith:

> *Behold here is wisdom, and let every man chose for himself until I come.* (D&C 37:4.)

Nephi outlines what one is free to choose. He says,

> *Wherefore, men are free according to the flesh; and all things are given them which are expedient unto man. And they are free to choose liberty and eternal life ... or to choose captivity and death.* (2 Nephi 2:27.)

Heavenly Father also gave unto man the right to act for himself, but he concluded that this could only be possible if he were enticed by good and evil. (2 Nephi 2:27.) He also indicated that man is to act and not to be acted upon. (2 Nephi 2:26)

> *All truth is independent in that sphere in which God has placed it, to act for itself, as all intelligence also, otherwise there is no existence.* (D&C 93:30)

> For the power is in them, wherein they are agents unto
> themselves.... (D&C 58:28)

> ...and becoming as Gods knowing good from evil, placing
> themselves in a state to act, or being placed in a state to act according to
> their wills and pleasures, whether to do evil or to do good. (Alma 12:31)

What one does or says is determined by what one thinks and
feels. Since each person is judged by his works, according to the
book of Revelation (Revelation 20:13.) it isn't surprising that we are
cautioned to watch our words, thoughts, and desires of the heart.
(Mosiah 4:30; D&C 137:9.) We cannot do an act without thinking first
and then desiring it. We cannot speak words without feeling and
thinking first. This is probably why the Savior counseled us to
love God, "with all thy heart and with all thy soul, and with all thy
mind." (Matthew 22:37.) In this counsel he included the mind, heart,
spirit, and body.

The world is mainly designed to appeal to the appetites of the
flesh. Movies, television, magazines, skiing, boating, world
travel, campers, hunting, fishing, cycles, sports, money, power,
success, recognition, romantic love, possessions, self-worth,
acceptance of others, and fear of man all are evidences of this.
However, these elements of life can be for the good of man if they
are seen through one's spiritual eyes. The world itself can help
one grow spiritually, rather than causing us to meet the lusts of
the flesh, if this is the desire of one's mind and heart. Each person
must decide which path he will tread.

Law of Sowing and Reaping

Apostle Paul told the Galatians that "whatsoever a man
soweth, that shall he also reap. For he that soweth to his flesh
shall of the flesh reap corruption; but he that soweth to the Spirit
shall of the Spirit reap life everlasting." (Galatians 6:7, 8; D&C 6:33.)

In order for one to grow spiritually, he must put into his mind
spiritual things. He must choose to pray unto God and exercise
faith. And faith is the substance of things hoped for—which takes

place in the imagination of the mind. In order to feel the direction of the Holy Ghost, one must place spiritual things in his mind and then in his heart fully believe in them. (Alma 32:28.) If one desires to reap spirituality he must seek after spiritual goals. The scriptures suggest various goals one could seek in the spiritual dimension.

> *Be ye therefore perfect, even as your Father which is in heaven is perfect.* (Matthew 5:48)
>
> *Seek ye first the kingdom of God and his righteousness.* (Matthew 6:33)
>
> *Labour ... for that meat which endureth unto everlasting life.* (John 6:27)
>
> *Before ye seek for riches, seek ye for the Kingdom of God.* (Jacob 2:18)
>
> *Seek for me diligently and ye shall find me.* (D&C 46:8)
>
> *Seek, and ye shall find.* (Matthew 7:7)
>
> *Pray unto the Father with all energy of heart, that ye may be filled with this love.* (Moroni 7:48)

As one seeks after spirituality he will reap it and thereby become centered in God and not in man. By doing so he will be able to understand the adversities of this life and use them for greater spiritual growth. When others ridicule him or find fault unjustly, he will draw upon this inner spiritual strength and thereby be able to love them and help them. He will have learned how to control his feelings and desires, regardless of the environment.

Who then is responsible for how I feel? Do others *make* me mad or do I allow others to control my mind and therefore how I will feel? The Lord has made each of us master of our own destiny— including our actions, thoughts, and feelings.

Revelation and Prayer

In what dimensions of one's being do prayer and revelation take place?

Ask and ye shall receive (This is accomplished in the imagination and the heart.)

Seek and ye shall find (So is this.)

Knock and it shall be opened unto you. (Matthew 7:7.) (After one has asked and sought for revelation he can act in the physical world and bring his prayer into being.)

One who doesn't pray with real intent will never receive an answer from heaven. One must pray in faith, believing he will receive, *which takes the full use of one's mind and feelings of the heart.* Heavenly Father knows what one needs before he asks, (Matthew 6:8.) but it takes all the energy of the heart for one to have the faith to bring about the answers to his prayers. This denotes that concentration is needed; that is, one needs to run the prayer through his mind and heart many times in order to reach a level of faith for its realization.

How does Heavenly Father answer our prayers and give us revelation?

> *Yea, behold I will tell you in your* **mind** *and in your* **heart,** *by the Holy Ghost, which shall come upon you and which shall dwell in your* **heart.** (D&C 8:2.)

The Savior gives us further insight on how to pray and feel revelation.

> *Behold, you have not understood; you have supposed that I would give it unto you, when you took no* **thought** *save it was to ask me.* [It doesn't sound like the heart or imagination was involved in this prayer.]
>
> *But, behold, I say unto you, that you must study it out in your* **mind;** *then you must ask me if it be right and if it is right I will cause that your* **bosom** [heart] *shall burn within you; therefore, you shall* **feel** *that it is right.*
>
> *But if it be not right you shall have no such* **feeling,** *but you shall have a stupor of* **thought** *that shall cause you to* **forget** *the thing which is wrong.* (D&C 9:7-9.)

Alma also reviews what happens to man as he seeks for the truth and receives direction from heaven.

> *It must needs to be the word is good . . . for it beginneth to enlarge my soul* [spiritual]; *yea, it beginneth to enlighten my understanding* [mind], *yea it beginneth to be delicious* [heart] *to me.* (Alma 32:28.)

How to Control the Mind

The mind can only entertain one thought at a time; therefore, if one sets his mind on a goal and becomes emotional about it, it seems that he will find it easier to make decisions, as well as to control his mind. When a person wants to buy a home and he gets excited about it, the mind is able to see all the "for-sale signs" along the street. If a person wants a new car, his mind will attract that brand of car, which previously went unnoticed.

According to Nephi, one has a choice between two goals: liberty and eternal life or captivity and death. (2 Nephi 2:27.) If I choose to walk in the strait and narrow path and gain eternal life, my perception and reaction to a negative situation could be quite different than if I had not set that goal. For example, if someone condemned me, found fault with me, or embarrassed me, and I had no spiritual goal, these negative feelings would remain with me for some time. But if my mind and heart were centered on God and Christ and I felt the companionship of the Holy Ghost, then I would react differently. When the negative feelings were felt, I would feel the Spirit leave and would then choose to think of God, forgive the people involved, and feel the peace and joy again, as the Spirit returned. How would I do it? By changing the thoughts of my mind from the negative circumstance to the love I have for my Father in Heaven. If my feelings for Heavenly Father are stronger than my feelings of rejection, then love for this person who rejects me can dominate my being and I will be in control again.

As one develops a closer spiritual relationship with Heavenly Father, these emotions become stronger and stronger. And as the emotions gradually grow stronger, it becomes easier to overcome negative experiences, by changing the focus of one's mind to dwell on God and his love.

Another example could be with the same problem of rejection. But this time, while the person was in the midst of these negative feelings, someone gave him a $1,000,000. I am sure his feelings would change quickly. What produces the change? His mind changed from the negative situation to the positive scene of spending the money — and the emotions followed the mind. That is, the excitement of having a million dollars and all the things one can do with it would dominate the feelings of rejection. He would not repeatedly be running negative feelings through his mind and heart, which is necessary if one is going to sustain negative feelings.

Setting goals that have great importance can help a person control his mind and heart, and what he says and does. For example, a person desires with all his heart and mind to gain eternal life; he thus spends several minutes each day imagining himself receiving the gift of eternal life from the Savior. He has set many other goals, but each relates to this all-consuming goal. Here are a few of them: full-time mission, temple marriage, walk by the Spirit daily, increase in knowledge and intelligence, keep physically fit, love all persons, serve God when called, and become financially independent.

What effect would these spiritual goals have on the following actions?

If telling a lie will help him gain his goal of increased income, what would he decide? When his body demanded more food, which wasn't necessary, would he give in to the flesh or would he seek to become like God and bring the appetites, desires, and passions of the flesh under control? As he studied the scriptures, would he study to get it done, or use this time to feel God's Spirit? As he felt the joy of the Holy Ghost, would he go to an R- or X-rated movie, where he would lose it? When someone found fault with him and he felt low, would he seek the help of God or would he reject himself and others? As he carried a prayer in his heart throughout the day, would he be patient or impatient? As adversities came into his life, would he humbly seek God and overcome, or would he reject all spiritual things and feel like a failure? When he did home teaching would he do it so the elder's quorum president would feel good about him or because of the love he felt for his Father in heaven?

It is easy to answer the above questions correctly. The problem is living in this world and doing all the things one knows is right, and having enough time and energy to do all that one knows is right. This leads us into our suggested solution, and that is how to keep all the commandments today and enjoy it.

How to Keep All the Commandments

When I am conducting firesides or workshops I frequently ask what it takes for one to qualify for the celestial kingdom. The answer that is given most often is that one must keep all the commandments. Then I ask, "Who here is keeping all the commandments?" No one raises their hand. Therefore, it looks like no one will qualify for the celestial kingdom. But this cannot be—there must be something wrong with our perception, since most Latter-day Saints have negative feelings when they are told they must keep all the commandments in order to be saved. Let's see if we can clear up our perception, so we can feel peace as we press forward in the strait and narrow path and keep all the commandments.

First, let us review some of the scriptures on the importance of the commandments:

> *And thus we see that the commandments of God must be fulfilled.* (1 Nephi 17:3.)

> *Nevertheless, he that repents and does the commandments of the Lord shall be forgiven.* (D&C 1:32.)

> *If ye love me keep my commandments.* (John 14:15.)

For if you keep my commandments you shall receive of his fulness, and be glorified in one as I am in the Father. (D&C 93:20.)

For behold, it is not meet that I should command in all things; for he that is compelled in all things, the same is a slothful and not a wise servant; wherefore he receiveth no reward. (D&C 58:26.)

Ye shall diligently keep the commandments of the Lord your God, and his testimonies, and his statutes, which he hath commanded thee. (Deuteronomy 6:17.)

Therefore to him that knoweth to do good, and doeth it not, to him it is a sin. (James 4:17.)

For whosoever shall keep the whole law, and yet offend in one point, he is guilty of all. (James 2:10.)

If thou lovest me thou shalt serve me and keep all my commandments. (D&C 42:29.)

ASSIGNMENT

Please take the time and do each step as suggested before going on to the next. This solution needs to be experienced and not just understood.

Step One

Take a sheet of paper and list all the laws, ordinances, and commandments you feel are necessary for you to qualify for the celestial kingdom.

Note: Do the above under the guidance of the Holy Ghost. See Appendix A for one group's list.

Step Two

Ask Heavenly Father to help you check off those items on your list that you are currently living, or have completed. (For example, baptism, tithing, Word of Wisdom, sacrament meeting attendance, etc., could be checked off).

Step Three

Ask Heavenly Father to help you check off those items on your list which you need not be concerned about for the next 30-90 days, even though you may not be fulfilling them currently.

Note: Will Heavenly Father really tell us not to work on a law or commandment? If I am sick will he approve my missing sacrament meeting? If my wife is ready to walk out and leave me should I stay home from priesthood meeting and try to save my marriage? If my neighbor's son was put in jail this morning and I am asked to go and comfort him, would it be all right to miss priesthood meeting? In the eyes of some others it may not be right, but God would approve.

Let me show you how to carry out *Step Three.*

First: Find out how much free time you have each day to work on more commandments, etc. For example, each day you might do the following:

> Sleep — 8 hours
> Work — 8 hours
> Eat, dress, etc. — 2 hours
> Interruptions — 2 hours
> Scripture study,
> Family home evening, — 2 hours
> Garden, etc.
> T.V., newspaper   — 2 hours

Total hours: 24

In that schedule you can find one or two hours per day that you can work on keeping more laws and commandments, assuming you have any energy left.

Second: Ask Heavenly Father to help you select those laws, ordinances, commandments, or suggestions that would be of most worth to you and would most help your family's spiritual growth over the next 30-90 days. (Keep in mind how much time you have to work on them.)

Third: Those items on your list that have not been checked off or selected are the ones Heavenly Father suggests you not worry about in the next 30–90 days. It's basically that simple.

Step Four

Take the list of commandments that you are going to work on over the next 30–90 days and put them in order of importance. If you have five items, find out which one would be of most worth to your spiritual growth right now, which one would be second, and so forth.

Step Five

Use the formula of prayer to receive guidance on the various ways you can live these laws and enjoy them. As you receive many suggestions to implement the commandments, ask Heavenly Father to help you prioritize them.

Step Six

Now you are ready to work on commandment number one and activity number one for today. *But first, let us review the purpose of the commandments,* so we can maximize our efforts.

Purpose of the Commandments

One can do all the commandments and still not gain salvation. The *focus* must not be on the commandment but on gaining salvation and growing spiritually. The commandments are designed to effect spiritual growth. Therefore, if one's priority is studying the scriptures this month, the intent is to help him grow spiritually. If he does scripture reading and checks it off his list, but doesn't seek spiritual guidance and doesn't feel love from Heavenly Father, it is of little value. In fact, the focus in this case would only be on his feeling better because he is doing a commandment. His guilt feelings would decrease; he would feel better as a person of worth. But all of this would negatively effect his spiritual growth, because his feelings of self-worth are being built upon worldly performance, which is a sandy foundation.

If a person can effect spiritual growth by doing one more commandment, it is not necessary that he do ten more. In fact, if he tried to improve in ten more today, it would negate his spiritual growth. I know people who try to improve in ten commandments all at once, along with work, exercise, sleep, Church commitments, family activities, yard work, and on and on—and all they accomplish is to become frustrated and discouraged.

In fact, if they had watched closely, they would have known when the Spirit left them. Their focus was on *doing more commandments,* not effecting spiritual growth.

Let us assume your 30-90 day inspired list was as follows:

1. Scripture study
2. Family home evening
3. Temple work
4. Gardening
5. Life history

If you concentrated on scripture study and that was the only one you improved on over the next 30 days, meaning you felt spiritual growth, would it help you when you got the chance to work on the other four items? Very definitely. Because of your spiritual growth it would help you have better family home evenings, provide increased spiritual energy to do temple work, help you feel greater love for Heavenly Father as you worked in the garden, and help you gain spiritual insight to record your life history. Therefore, as you did number one correctly, you also improved in all five areas.

Basic Philosophy: I may not be *doing* all the laws, ordinances, suggestions, and commandments today but I am *keeping* all the commandments today. The purpose of the commandments is to help one grow spiritually, to feel the influence of the Holy Ghost daily, to feel more spiritually alive and in tune with Heavenly Father. One will feel God's love for him and God's love for his fellowman. He will be patient, loving, giving, and most of all he will feel at peace. No longer will he use the commandments to measure his worth, but he will feel the commandments are the steps he can use to draw closer to his Heavenly Father. He will come to love the laws of God and seek to use them to grow spiritually as he is taught by the Spirit. He will not measure his progress by comparing his performance or lack of performance with that of others, for he will know each person can achieve salvation as each seeks the guidance of the Spirit. This basic philosophy was taught by the Savior when he counseled the Pharisees, "The Sabbath was made for man, and not man for the Sabbath." (Mark 2:27.) The same can be said of the gospel itself, and of all the commandments.

Step Seven

Each week, review the list with Heavenly Father to see if the priority is changed. If it hasn't changed then continue to work on your list of activities which will help you experience the joy of keeping that law. When you attend meetings, or read the *Ensign* magazine, or listen to conference, and you hear something that affects your salvation, make sure it is on your list. If not, then add it on. Next, check with Heavenly Father to see if it ought to be on your priority list for your spiritual progression. If you do not feel impressed that it ought to replace one of your priority commandments, then keep working on your list as before.

By following these steps, one will feel good about keeping all the commandments, because he is being directed by the Spirit. He will not fear any new thoughts given by the Brethren on doing what the Lord says. And when someone says to keep all the commandments, he will feel peace and joy in his heart, for he knows that all commandments are given to help him grow spiritually (D&C 29:35.) and prepare himself to dwell in the celestial kingdom. (D&C 88:34-39.) We have this life and the Millennium to learn to keep all the laws, ordinances, suggestions, and commandments necessary to become exalted. The key of this life is to press forward in the strait and narrow path under the influence of the Holy Ghost, and by doing so we will walk in the light and avoid spiritual darkness.

*If you keep not my commandments, the love of the Father shall not
continue with you, therefore you shall walk in darkness. (D&C 95:12.)*

The commandments are given to help us draw near unto God

and abide in his love. (John 15:10.) They are to prepare us to be lifted up at the last days (D&C 5:22, 35.) and be forgiven. (D&C 58:42, 43.) The commandments were not designed to be used to condemn ourselves or others. (James 4:11, 12.) Those who fear the commandments do not see clearly and have developed a confused perception of the gospel. The commandments are desirable, and they bring joy and peace into one's life. To live the commandments is to know God and his Son. Heavenly Father does not ask us to keep the commandments so He can love us more, but so we can feel his love more. (John 15: 10.)

I know members who are divorced and are raising children. They are working eight hours per day earning a living; then they come home and work another four to six hours, do Church assignments, and then condemn themselves because they are not keeping their journals. Heavenly Father is greatful if they can endure the load of earning a living and raising the children, let alone trying to jog, plant a garden, write their life histories, do genealogy, attend the temple, and do community service.

Satan keeps pointing out all the laws, ordinances, suggestions, and commandments we are not living, as if it were possible for us to *do* them all today. The Savior suggests that we seek to grow spiritually, and by doing so our light will grow brighter and brighter until the perfect day. (D&C 50:24.) Spiritual growth is a process, and the laws, ordinances, suggestions, and commandments help us to grow spiritually. As we concentrate on improving in keeping the commandments and walking by the Holy Ghost, we are in the strait and narrow path that leads unto life.

If one is trying to "do a perfect" by telling himself that he should do all the laws, ordinances, suggestions, and commandments, and suggestions today, does this attitude bring peace and joy or anxiety and frustration? He who expects himself to "do a perfect *today*" is relying on himself to do it—and it is impossible for him to do it alone. He has set an expectation level to jump over, rather than seeking God's counsel on his spiritual growth. (Jacob 4:10.)

Those who seek to improve by the Spirit testify of peace and joy as they journey up the path. Those who expect "perfection today" testify of feelings of inadequacy, frustration, anger, and other negative feelings. May each of us seek to be directed by the Spirit and bring joy and peace into our hearts, which we so richly deserve.

Section IV

PERCEPTIONS THAT AFFECT MY SPIRITUAL GROWTH

During my years as an ecclesiastical officer, it became obvious to me that many members of the Church were struggling spiritually. Some were struggling in their marital relations, some with their sense of self-worth to the point of feeling incapable of handling Church and family responsibilities. Some were feeling that the Church was a burden, not a blessing. After attending a Church meeting, these members would feel discouraged rather than spiritually uplifted. They knew the Church was true, but doubted their chance of ever qualifying for the celestial kingdom. After reviewing the long list of things to do in order to become exalted, a few members even wondered why they should try anymore.

Contrast the above concerns with the scriptures, which indicate a different feeling for one who lives the gospel:

Adam fell that men might be; and men are, that they might have joy.
(2 Nephi 2:25)

> *Come unto me, all ye that labour and are heavy laden, and I will give you rest. . . .* (Matt. 11:28, 30)
>
> *I am come that they might have life, and that they might have it more abundantly.* (John 10:10)

Apostle George Q. Cannon testified of a happier state in this life if one lives the gospel:

> I will tell you a rule by which you may know the spirit of God from the spirit of evil. The spirit of God always produces joy and satisfaction of mind.
>
> When you have that spirit you are happy; when you have another spirit, you are not happy. The spirit of doubt is the spirit of the evil one; it produces uneasiness and other feelings that interfere with happiness and peace.
>
> It is your privilege, and it ought to be your rule, my brethren and sisters, to always have peace and joy in your hearts. When you wake in the morning and your spirits are disturbed, you may know there is some spirit or influence that is not right. You should never leave your bedchambers until you can get that calm, serene, and happy influence that flows from the presence of the spirit of God, and that is the fruit of that spirit. So during the day, you are apt to get disturbed, angry and irritated about something. You should stop, and not allow that influence to prevail or have place in your heart. . . .
>
> We of all people should be happy and joyful. When the clouds seem the darkest and most threatening, and as though the storm is ready to burst upon us with all its fury, we should be calm, serene and undisturbed, for if we have the faith we profess to have, we know that God is in the storm, in the cloud, or in the threatened danger, and that He will not let it come upon us only as far as it is necessary for our good and for our salvation; and we should, even then, be calm and rejoice before God and praise Him. . . I know some will say, this is folly and enthusiasm; but notwithstanding this idea, I know that

there is a power in the religion of Jesus Christ to sustain
men even under these circumstances, and they can rejoice
in them. [1]

The purpose of this section is to review several principles of the
gospel which bring joy and happiness into one's life regardless of
his present conditions. It has been my experience that when I am
not happy I have made two mistakes. First, my *understanding* of a
gospel principle which was creating a burden for me was really
misunderstood. Second, my *application* of the misunderstood principle
was bringing me unrest and dissatisfaction. When I came to
understand the principle of the gospel correctly and applied it in
my life as Heavenly Father directed, I began to receive the joy
Brother Cannon testified of.

President McKay answers the question about what it is that
motivates a person to grow spiritually:

> There is in man not an instinct, but a divinity that
> strives to push him onward and upward: this sense or
> feeling is present with every normal human being ready
> to perfect it, in response to which all men should be
> earnestly and sincerely engaged in the search for and
> development of *spiritual peace and freedom.*
>
> Spirituality is best expressed in doing, not in dreaming.
>
> Every noble impulse; every unselfish expression of
> love; every brave suffering for the right; *every surrender of
> self to something higher than self;* every loyalty to an ideal; every
> unselfish devotion to principle; every helpfulness to
> humanity; every act of self-control; every fine courage of
> the soul, undefeated by pretense or policy, but by being,
> doing, and living of good for the very good's sake — *that is
> spirituality.* [2]

---

1. George Q. Cannon, *Journal of Discourses,* 15:375.
2. David O. McKay, *Treasures of Life,* (Deseret Book Co., 1962,) p. 363.

Chapter Eleven

Gospel Perceptions

---

1. Demands of Justice

YOU HAVE DECIDED to jump off a two-story building. I do not know why you have decided to jump, but it does not make any difference anyway — the consequences will be the same. You find a suitable building, climb the stairs, and finally reach the top. You notice that it is much higher than you had imagined, but there is a soft lawn below. Your thoughts are interrupted by the blowing of a whistle of the mill in the distance. It is 8:00 a.m., and many people have started their routine for the day.

You look around to see if anyone is nearby. You notice that there is no one, and everything is clear. Next, you check to see where the various trees and bushes are located below, and you adjust your jumping position accordingly. You make certain no protrusions of the building will get in your way. Finally, you evaluate the wind to make sure it will not interfere with your journey, and conclude you are ready.

After the final check, you jump. It is a thrilling experience as you travel downward. It is exhilarating to feel the wind over your whole being, the loss of control, and the quickness of the trip. The only problem with the experience is the landing part. You land, luckily, on your feet, then your side, with your arm helping to break the fall. You then feel great pain and pass out.

In the hospital you awaken and are told by the nurse that you are really lucky. You only broke your ankles, sprained your back, tore some ligaments in your arm, and broke a few ribs. And, she assures you, in a few months you should be as good as new.

The results of this experience were administered under the demands of justice. That is, when one jumps from the top of a two-story building and creates trauma for his body, it usually means the following:

a. He has complied with the laws to break both ankles, sprain the back, pull ligaments in the arm, and break some ribs.
b. He may hurt for the rest of his life because of this decision to jump.
c. Some parts of the body may not heal completely or as good as new.
d. When he kneels to pray it could cause pain in his back and create difficulty in being relaxed while praying.
e. This may affect the kind of job he can do in the future.
f. He may be limited in the fun activities he can participate in.

But the painful results of this experience do *not* mean the following:

a. Heavenly Father does not love me and this is why I hurt so much.
b. I am no good because I made a mistake.
c. My hurting is the result of my unworthiness, not just from my mistake.
d. God does not love me. How do I know? Because he would remove my pain if he loved me.

Some Have Been Tricked

Some people have been taught that God does not love them unless they always perform correctly or righteously. Life's experiences seem to support that teaching: Whey they sinned they felt so much pain, unworthiness, and discouragement that they knew God did not love them. When they kept the commandments with all their hearts they felt joy, happiness, peace, and other good feelings about themselves, since they felt God's love for them.

In fact, when they performed well, others liked them, admired them, and said good things about them. When they broke a law they not only felt bad inside, but others tended to put them down. They knew if others really knew them deep inside they would not really like them.

Are these conclusions correct? They have been tricked. The demands of justice have nothing to do with our *spiritual worth.* Let us understand more clearly the purpose of the demands of justice.

What Is Justice?

Justice means that the results of our actions are based on a fairness to all parties. The results are always the same, regardless of who keeps or breaks the law. It is essential that we know that God is just with each of us, regardless of our position in life. This in taught in the *Lectures on Faith:*

> Could man exercise faith in God so as to obtain eternal life unless he believed that God was no respector of persons? He could not; because without this idea he could not certainly know that it was his privilege so to do, and in consequence of this doubt his faith could not be sufficiently strong to save him. [1]

The phrase "demands of justice" denotes that there is no impartiality. It requires that the same results occur regardless of

---

1. *Lectures on Faith,* pp. 38–39.

who keeps or breaks the law. If a prophet chose not to pray he would not receive revelation — nor would you or I if we chose not to pray. If the prophet wanted to keep in good physical condition, he would have to exercise and live the laws of health. If one desires to have a good vocabulary it is necessary to practice and pay the price, regardless of his position in life. The demands of justice see to it that if one lives a good life he will be rewarded. (D&C 130:20-21.)

Purpose of the Demands of Justice

First, the purpose of the principle of justice is to help remove the doubts within us so we can have complete faith in God. Joseph Smith, as reported in the *Lectures on Faith,* said:

> It is also necessary, in order to the exercise of faith in God unto life and salvation, that men should have the idea of the existence of the attribute justice in him; for without the idea of the existence of the attribute justice in the Deity, men could not have confidence sufficient to place themselves under his guidance and direction; for they would be filled with fear and doubt lest the judge of all the earth would not do right, and thus fear and doubt, existing in the mind, would preclude the possibility of the exercise of faith in him for life and salvation; but when the idea of the existence of the attribute justice in the Deity is fairly planted in the mind, it leaves no room for doubt to get into the heart, and the mind is enabled to cast itself upon the Almighty without fear and without doubt, and with the most unshaken confidence, believing that the Judge of all the earth will do right. [2]

Second, the demands of justice are so designed as to see that the consequences follow from what one chooses to sow. If one sows seeds of corn he will reap corn. If he chooses to sow seeds of kindness he receives kindness. Like attracts like. (D&C 88:40.) If one chooses to walk in spiritual darkness he will reap the

---

2. *Lectures on Faith,* p. 43.

consequences. If one jumps off a two-story building he will fall to the ground with a thud. We do not need to be concerned about whether the consequences will follow the act; it will happen automatically. One doesn't have to expend any energy to have the consequence follow, the Department of Heavenly Justice will see to all the details on our behalf.

Third, justice is designed to bring us back into the presence of Heavenly Father. When one follows the path unto life, he receives blessings, as administered by the laws of justice.

> *And again, verily I say unto you, that which is governed by the law is also preserved by the law and perfected and sanctified by the same.* (D&C 88:34.)

And when one chooses to walk in spiritual darkness the consequences will follow as the night follows day; there is no escape. As one understands his purpose for being on this earth it becomes clear how the demands of justice help him to come back into the presence of God.

As one walks in the strait and narrow path he reaps joy, peace, and love. When he chooses to walk in darkness, he experiences pain, suffering, and despair. He learns which way is correct and which will bring him joy. If there were no pain or suffering when one turned from God, then he would not know until it was too late that he was on the wrong path and his days of probation would be wasted. When his premortal life can be remembered again he will see his mistake, but then it will be too late. As pain is felt when one places his hand on a hot stove, which is a warning that it is not good to leave one's hand on the stove, so do the demands of justice warn us of danger when we turn our hearts from God.

Penalties Are Not Overly Harsh

The penalties that are affixed to breaking the laws are designed to help us change our ways, not to destroy us. For example, if one runs a stop sign there is a $50 fine as a penalty. However, this does not always teach people never to run a stop sign. This would certainly stop that person from doing it again.

If God were to use penalties so severe it would violate the great law of free agency, it might prevent me from reaching the goal of becoming like God. Therefore, the penalties of justice must not put me out of the race, but simply put a greater load on my back until I learn that it is easier to run the race of life without the extra burdens which come from the consequences of sin.

Mercy Can Meet the Demands of Justice, If ...

Since we all have sinned and come short of the glory of God, we have violated the laws of heaven and therefore must be cast out. No unclean thing can dwell in the presence of God. Since the wages of sin is death, we all have or will experience a physical and spiritual death. A spiritual death is to be cut off from the presence of God. (Alma 42:7.)

Remember, mercy (God) cannot rob justice. On the other hand, *the demands of justice cannot be so severe as to stop us from becoming like God.* Therefore, a way was provided so that the demands of justice could be satisfied. This plan provided that God, being merciful, would help us — *if* we fulfilled certain conditions:

> *And now, there was no means to reclaim men from this fallen state, which man had brought upon himself because of his own disobedience: Therefore, according to justice, the plan of redemption could not be brought about, only on conditions of repentance of men in this probationary state, yea, this preparatory state; for except it were for these conditions, mercy could not take effect except it should destroy the work of justice. Now the work of justice could not be destroyed; if so, God would cease to be God. And thus we see that all mankind were fallen, and they were in the grasp of God, which consigned them forever to be cut off from His presence. And now the plan of mercy could not be brought about except an atonement should be made: Therefore God himself atoneth for the sins of the world, to bring about the plan of mercy, to appease the demands of justice, that God might be a perfect, just God, and a merciful God also. Now, repentance could not come*

> *unto man except there was a punishment, which also was eternal as the life of the soul should be, affixed opposite to the plan of happiness, which was as eternal also as the life of the soul.* (Alma 42:12-16.)

As we read the above, we can see the magnitude of the stakes involved in the contest of life. Two conditions were set. First, repentance can bring us back into the presence of God and a state of joy and happiness. Or second, if we do not repent the demands of justice will claim all her own and punishment will be carried out. For the Lord says that "a punishment...should be affixed...which was eternal also as the life of the soul."

Jesus Christ can help balance the scales of justice if we qualify ourselves for his gift.

> *But God ceaseth not to be God, and mercy claimeth the penitent, and mercy cometh because of the atonement; and the atonement bringeth to pass the resurrection of the dead; and the resurrection of the dead bringeth back men to the presence of God, and thus they are restored into his presence, to be judged according to their works, according to the law and justice.* (Alma 42:23.)

We are cast out through violating a law; however, through Christ we are brought back into the presence of God to be judged.

Conclusion

We have been placed upon this earth to gain a body and see if we can qualify to come back into the presence of God. He has given us certain laws (commandments) which indicate the steps necessary to qualify for the celestial kingdom.

Each law has its consequence. Through our experiences we come to learn good from evil. Each of us can testify of many good laws and their blessings. We also can testify of the consequence of walking in spiritual darkness. And even as we repented and sought the light, we have seen that many of those consequences continued with us — it takes time and effort to overcome the effects of walking in spiritual darkness. All of these experiences have been for our good and growth. They were designed to help us return unto Heavenly Father and become like him.

2. Judging Yourself

*But with me it is a very small thing that I should be judged of you, or
of man's judgment: yea, I judge not mine own self. For I know nothing
by myself; yet am I not hereby justified: but he that judgeth me is the
Lord. Therefore judge nothing before the time, until the Lord come, who
both will bring to light the hidden things of darkness and will make
manifest the counsels of the hearts: and then shall every man have
praise of God.* (1 Corinthians 4:3-5.)

Apostle Paul suggested that we refrain from judging ourselves
until the Savior comes. If we judge ourselves unrighteously, we
do it by man's judgment. If we judge righteously, we must do it
with the Spirit of God.

*And now, verily, verily, I say unto thee, put your trust in that Spirit
which leadeth to do good, yea, to do justly, to walk humbly, to judge
righteously: and this is my Spirit.* (D&C 11:12.)

To judge is all right as long as it is done righteously:

*Now these are the words which Jesus taught his disciples that they
should say unto the people, judge not unrighteously, that ye be not
judged: but judge righteous judgment.* (Matthew 7:1-2.)

Neal A. Maxwell cautions us:

Some of us who would not chastise a neighbor for his
frailties have a field day with our own. Some of us stand
before no more harsh a judge than ourselves, a judge who
stubbornly refuses to admit much happy evidence and
who cares nothing for due process. Fortunately, the Lord
loves us more than we love ourselves.[3]

We should rely on God's judgment of how we are doing and not
on our own judgment or "man's judgment." How do we know if
we are clean and pure before him? By feeling the presence of the
Holy Ghost. One cannot be unclean and have the companionship
of the Holy Ghost.

---

3. Neal A. Maxwell, *Conference Report*, Oct. 1976, p. 14.

We remove ourselves from the influence of Satan by relying on the Holy Ghost to judge us, rather than relying on others or even ourselves. By allowing heaven to indicate our standing and worthiness, we remove ourselves from the lasting effects of the opinions of others. This helps us learn to love others unconditionally, making us more Godlike in our relationships with other people.

What does it mean to judge?

It means to reach an opinion or conclusion about someone or something. *To condemn yourself or another is not accurate unless you are doing it with the companionship of the Holy Ghost or the Spirit of Christ.* Brigham Young suggested:

> Think of this, brethren and sisters, write it down, that you may refresh your memories with it; carry it with you and look at it often. If I judge my brethren and sisters, unless I judge them by the revelation of Jesus Christ, I have not the Spirit of Christ; if I had, I should judge no man. [4]

Read Moroni 7:15-19.

What is the purpose of judging?

1. We need to judge good from evil. (Moroni 7:15-18.)

2. We need to judge righteously. (Alma 41:14.)

3. We need to make choices (2 Nephi 2:27) and to act. (D&C 93:30.)

4. How about when we use the laws of God to measure our progress?

5. How about when we use the law to determine whether we are a good person or not, or whether our brother is living righteously?

> *Speak not evil one of another, brethren. He that speaketh evil of his brother, and judgeth his brother, speaketh evil of the law, and judgeth*

---

4. Brigham Young, *Discourses of Brigham Young,* pp. 277-78.

*the law; but if thou judge the law, thou art not a doer of the law, but a
judge. . . . There is one lawgiver, who is able to save and to destroy; who
art thou, that judgest another.* (James 4:11-12.)

6. When one judges another what is he judging? The other
person's spiritual worth? His performance? His worthiness for
gifts?

   Someone makes only 40 percent of his home teaching visits
consistently. If we say John does a poor job in home teaching,
are we correct? Is John still worthy of a temple recommend? Is
he still a good person? Yes, we can say that his performance is
poor in home teaching, but this judgment does not affect my
feeling that John is a good person.

7. We have been counseled to be ready to meet God, through
death, at any given moment. Does having this sense of
readiness entail any judging on our part? By what measure do
you measure this judgment? Perfection or progression? How
can you tell you are progressing on schedule?

8. How do we feel when someone else judges us unrighteously?
Rotten? Why do we choose to feel that way about ourselves?
There is only one person qualified to judge my progression and
that is Christ. Why would someone else want to judge me? So
they can feel better?

Be Patient with Self

Elder Marvin J. Ashton counsels us:

   May I ask you to think with me for a few moments
about patience with self. Have more patience with
yourself — more self-understanding. I would plead that
we understand it is not our role to be self-condemning. I
like to think when we are taught "judge not that ye be not
judged," that it has direct reference to us and our
relationship with ourselves. We should not judge
ourselves. We should teach ourselves patience — patience

to believe in ourselves, patience to motivate ourselves, patience to believe that God and I can do it. [5]

3. Guilt Feelings

As reviewed in chapter twelve, one who walks in spiritual darkness suffers many consequences. That is, when one is found guilty under the demands of justice, he will suffer the withdrawal of the light of Christ. This withdrawal of the light of Christ brings spiritual suffering.

> *. . . Their souls were miserable, being cut off from the presence of the Lord.* (Alma 42:11.)

> *. . . Lest you suffer these punishments of which in the smallest, yea, even in the least degree you have tasted at the time I withdrew my Spirit.* (D&C 19:20.)

Lucy Mack Smith, Joseph Smith's mother, relates what happened when the Lord withdrew his Spirit:

> At eight o'clock we set the victuals on the table, as we were expecting him every moment. We waited till nine, and he came not — till ten, and he was not there — till eleven, still he did not make his appearance. But at half past twelve we saw him walking with a slow and measured tread towards the house, his eyes fixed thoughtfully upon the ground. On coming to the gate, he stopped, instead of passing through, and got upon the fence, and sat there some time with his hat drawn over his eyes. At length he entered the house. Soon after which we sat down to the table, Mr. Harris with the rest. He took up his knife and fork as if he were going to use them, but immediately dropped them. Hyrum, observing this, said, "Martin, why do you not eat; are you sick?" Upon which Mr. Harris pressed his hands upon his temples, and cried out in a tone of deep anquish, "Oh, I have lost my soul! I have lost my soul!"

---

5. Marvin J. Ashton, *Speeches of the Year — 1972-73*, p. 104.

Joseph, who had not expressed his fears till now, sprang from the table, exclaiming, "Martin, have you lost that manuscript? Have you broken your oath, and brought down condemnation upon my head as well as your own?"

"Yes; it is gone," replied Martin, "and I know not where."

"Oh, my God!" said Joseph, clinching his hands. "All is lost! all is lost! What shall I do? I have sinned — it is I who tempted the wrath of God. I should have been satisfied with the first answer which I received from the Lord; for he told me that it was not safe to let the writing go out of my possession." He wept and groaned, and walked the floor continually.

At length he told Martin to go back and search again.

"No"; said Martin, "it is all in vain; for I have ripped open beds and pillows; and I know it is not there."

"Then must I," said Joseph, "return with such a tale as this? I dare not do it. And how shall I appear before the Lord? Of what rebuke am I not worthy from the angel of the Most High?"

I besought him not to mourn so, for perhaps the Lord would forgive him, after a short season of humiliation and repentance. But what could I do to comfort him, when he saw all the family in the same situation of mind as himself; for sobs and groans, and the most bitter lamentations filled the house. However, Joseph was more distressed than the rest, as he better understood the consequences of disobedience. And he continued pacing back and forth, meantime weeping and grieving, until about sunset, when, by persuasion, he took a little nourishment.[6]

The purpose of guilt feelings is to warn us that we are leaving the light of Christ and turning unto darkness. These feelings are like the negative feedback that guides a missile. That is, whenever

---

6. Lucy Mack Smith, *History of Joseph Smith*, pp. 127–29, 132.

the missile starts to leave the path that leads to the target, a signal is emitted that causes a correction of the missile's flight. If the missile's system concentrated on the negative signal it would leave the path permanently. Instead, it reacts to the negative signal by getting back on course.

Some people, when they feel those guilt feelings caused by the withdrawal of the Spirit, humble themselves before the Lord and turn back unto the light. Some use the guilt feelings to put themselves down so they feel worthless, thereby moving quickly into spiritual darkness. Still others justify themselves in their sin, shutting off the powers and love from heaven. These people are the hardest to help out of spiritual darkness. The Lord was referring to this group when he said, "The guilty taketh the truth to be hard, for it cutteth them to the very center." (1 Nephi 16:2.) But if one chooses to remain in spiritual darkness and not repent, the demands of justice will awaken his spiritual soul and he will feel the pains of guilt again at the last day.

> *Therefore if that man repenteth not, and remaineth and dieth an enemy to God, the demands of divine justice do awaken his immortal soul to a lively sense of his own guilt, which doth cause him to shrink from the presence of the Lord, and doth fill his breast with guilt, and pain, and anguish, which is like an unquenchable fire, whose flame ascendeth up forever and ever.* (Mosiah 2:38.)

An earthly father will chastise his son because he loves him, so will our Heavenly Father chastise us, so we will change our course and draw near unto him. We will not be offended when we feel these guilt feelings within our hearts, but will be thankful and turn back unto the light.

> *Verily, thus saith the Lord unto you whom I love, and whom I love I also chasten, that their sins may be forgiven, for with the chastisement I prepare a way for their deliverance in all things out of temptation, and I have loved you.* (D&C 95:1.)

We as sons and daughters of God can look at the withdrawal of the Spirit (guilt feelings) as an act of love, as a call from Heavenly

Father for us to return to his ways. Chastisement is necessary for each of us if we wish to come back into the presence of God. To bear it with gratitude is to see clearly the purpose of correction.

My people must be tried in all things, that they may be prepared to receive the glory that I have for them, even the glory of Zion; and he that will not bear chastisement is not worthy of my kingdom. (D&C 136:31.)

May we see clearly the purposes of God and see good in all things that come from above. May we remember that if one finds himself in darkness he is guilty of transgression. May we come to hate darkness so much that we will be greatful for the chastisements of the Lord in our behalf and return unto him.

4. Self-Atonement

Jesus Christ atoned for the sins of this world. That is, "As in Adam all die, even so in Christ shall all be made alive." (1 Corinthians 15:22.) As far as one's personal sins are concerned, Christ paid for all *repented* sins. (D&C 19:16.) If one chooses not to repent, then he must suffer even as Christ suffered. (D&C 19:17.) That is, one must atone for his own sins. In the nineteenth section of the Doctrine and Covenants, Christ pleads with us to repent and allow his suffering to be valid on our behalf. He does not want us to have to suffer as he has suffered. In fact, if one suffers for his own sins it will not bring the benefits and blessings one receives when he accepts the Savior's sacrifice.

Evidently many will have to pay for their own sins and suffer even as Christ suffered (because they refused to repent), and this self-atonement will bring some blessings. However, there is another form of self-atonement that produces no benefits for anyone, but only darkness and misery. Many unwisely perform this self-atonement when they make a mistake, or sin, or are rejected by others, or see their loved ones making mistakes. When these things happen this individual runs negative thoughts through his mind. He tells himself he is no good, worthless, a pain to everyone, and that he deserves what he is getting. Satan moves in and says, "If you were a good person, you would not have all of these problems." This, of course, is a lie, since we know that adversities come upon the good as well as the bad. (Matthew 7:25, 27.) If anyone finds anything good about this person, he will deny it in his mind. It seems that this person wants to punish himself for making a mistake, or failing in some facet of life; it is as if he was ordained by the heavens to inflict punishment upon his person mentally, emotionally, and physically, and as if one could get through this life without sinning or making a mistake. (Romans 3:23.)

The sad part is that this type of behavior does not bring repentance or forgiveness, nor does it lead one back into spiritual light. In fact, it accomplishes the opposite: it leads one farther into darkness. The more one does a self-atonement, the greater his suffering and the greater his darkness. God does not require this type of punishment in order for one to be forgiven.

> *Yea, even wo unto all ye workers of iniquity; repent, repent, for the Lord God hath spoken it!*
> *Behold, he sendeth an invitation unto all men, for the arms of mercy are extended towards them, and he saith: repent, and I will receive you.*
> (Alma 5:32–33.)

The gift of repentance and forgiveness requires that one recognize his responsibility for the sin and prepare himself to meet the demands of justice. (Alma 42:29-30.) The effects of sin may last for years as a person overcomes the mistake. But one needs hope, love, faith, and a nearness to God and his Son in order to overcome. A self-atonement takes one away from the Godhead and keeps him in spiritual darkness. We should take care never to put ourselves down or listen to the lies of Satan. These things are contrary to our spiritual worth, and stop us from being forgiving of self and others. Draw unto God through his Son, Jesus Christ. Repentance does not require one to do this kind of a self-atonement — EVER.

I remember a wife calling for an appointment, and it was

evident that she was very upset. Arrangements were made immediately. In the interview she said her husband was going to leave her for another woman. This couple had been active in the Church for years. She broke down and cried; she could not accept that this was happening to her.

I asked her if she had prayed about this situation with Heavenly Father. "Yes, I have," she said — in fact, she had spent over two hours in prayer.

I then asked her, "What did he tell you?"

She said, "He won't answer me!"

You see, the doors to heaven were closed because she knew that her husband would not consider leaving her if she were a good person (or so she thought). She did not like herself, which is what Satan had been telling her for the past several hours. She loved herself only when certain levels of performance were obtained.

We spent an hour and a half talking about prayer and feelings of self-worth. Then we got on our knees and had prayer. She saw the spiritual doors open as she came to feel good about herself. Then she felt the love of her Heavenly Father and this became a very choice experience for her.

She learned a great lesson and her marriage is now happy and stable; the Lord helped her through the steps to overcome this problem. Of course, her receiving answers to her prayers had nothing to do with whether or not Heavenly Father liked her. He is always there to help us when we prepare ourselves to receive his help.

5. But I Am Not a Good Parent Unless All My Children Turn Out Okay

If one chooses to feel good about his/her personal worth based upon being a good parent, then this is believing in conditional love. One's performance as a parent has nothing to do with one's spiritual worth. Heavenly Father loves me regardless of how my children turn out.

There is another misconception about being a good parent and how one's children turn out. That is, am I responsible to see that my children turn out okay? What is our responsibility to our children? As parents we have been commanded to teach our children and set the proper example:

> *And again, inasmuch as parents have children in Zion, or in any of her stakes which are organized, that teach them not to understand the doctrine of repentance, faith in Christ the Son of the living God, and of baptism and the gift of the Holy Ghost by the laying on of the hands, when eight years old, the sin be upon the heads of the parents.*
>
> *And they shall also teach their children to pray, and to walk uprightly before the Lord.* (D&C 68:25, 28.)

We have been counseled that "no other success can compensate for failure in the home." (President David O. McKay) Also, President Harold B. Lee said, "The greatest work we will ever do is within the walls of our own home."

Our salvation and exaltation are not contingent upon how our children turn out. Many prophets, like Adam, Jacob, Lehi, and Joseph Smith, had children under their care who still went astray. Even Heavenly Father had such children! These children were taught the gospel and the proper example was obviously set. But some children will not accept the gospel or do not desire to have Heavenly Father as their guide. Each child has his/her free agency. Each child must decide what, how, and when he/she will live each principle.

To answer the question of responsibility to our children, let us review the words of some of our leaders:

> The home is the teaching situation. Every father should talk to his sons, every mother to her daughters. Then it would leave them totally without excuse should they ignore the counsel they have received. [7]

---

7. Spencer W. Kimball, *Conference Report,* Oct. 1974, p. 8.

I believe we start to fail in the home when we give up on each other. We have not failed until we have quit trying. As long as we are working diligently with love, patience, and long-suffering, we are not classified as failures in the home. We only start to fail when we give up on a son, daughter, mother, or father. [8]

The greatest gift we can give our children is unconditional love, regardless of their performance. Love involves discipline, as well as tenderness, when moved upon by the Holy Ghost:

Reproving betimes with sharpness, when moved upon by the Holy Ghost; and then showing forth afterwards an increase of love toward him whom thou hast reproved, lest he esteem thee to be his enemy. (D&C 121:43.)

6. To the Wives of Leaders, Spiritually Drained

It has been my experience that this group of chosen sisters is particularly the ones who expect themselves to live perfectly. They expect themselves to not have negative feelings about the absence of their husbands, the phone calls, the feeling that they are last on their husband's list of important things, the overburdened feelings of raising the family, and the loss of spirituality when attending church meetings with fussy children.

The sad part is that when these feelings build up (and by the way, these feelings are normal for wives of most leaders), the sister will condemn herself because she assumes that if she was spiritual she would not have these feelings. She concludes that when she is tired from interacting with the seven children, feeling overburdened with the work, never having any time for herself, feeling a need for adult companionship, and seeing her husband go off to bury the dead, she still should feel great that her husband can help the afflicted. But she really has both negative and positive feelings under these circumstances — and this is normal.

---

8. Elder Marvin J. Ashton.

Next we will find the sweet woman getting the five little ones ready for sacrament meeting, driving the family to church with a desire to be spiritually uplifted, but never hearing a word because of serving the little ones. By the time church is over, she is spiritually drained and concludes something is wrong with her for having these negative feelings.

Elder Neal A. Maxwell gives the following caution:

> Now may I speak, not to the slackers in the kingdom, but to those who carry their own load and more; . . . who, though laboring devotedly in the kingdom, have recurring feelings of falling forever short.
>
> . . . The first thing to be said of this feeling of inadequacy is that it is normal . . . thus the feelings of inadequacy are common. So are the feelings of fatigue; hence, the needed warning about our becoming weary of well doing. (See D&C 64:33.) The scriptural advice: "Do not run faster or labor more than you have strength" (D&C 10:4.) suggest paced progress. [9]

My advice to these women would be to recognize and accept these feelings as normal. Heavenly Father expects you to handle them. This could mean that a counselor might bury the dead this week, while the husband stays home and meets some of your needs. It may mean that you need to leave church before all the meetings are over, when you feel spiritually drained, and put two or three kids to bed, so you can recover. Now, I know someone at church will suggest that you ought to set a better example, but remember you are choosing to do those things that will bring you closer to Heavenly Father. And to recognize that you have reached your limit and then take appropriate action is the best step to rebuild your spiritual reservoir.

Keep in mind that the most important relationship is your relationship with Heavenly Father. When your "sacrifice" has reached its limits, then it is time for recreation, for refreshing, for

---

9. Neal A. Maxwell, *Conference Report,* Oct. 1976, p. 14.

spiritual rebuilding. And choosing not to recognize when your spiritual limit has been reached is to choose spiritual disaster.

I remember one sister whose husband was a counselor in a bishopric. They had five children, all of whom were quite young. She was expecting another child and hadn't been feeling well all week. With great effort she got all the children ready for church and arrived on time, even though some of the children were tired and cranky. Halfway through sacrament meeting she could see that all was not well and her energy was gone. She concluded, after seeking Heavenly Father's approval, that for her spiritual sake and that of her children, she needed to go home and put the kids to bed. Later that evening she received a call inquiring about her leaving sacrament meeting early. After giving her an explanation, the sister said, "Well, I hope next time that you will be able to stay for *all* the meetings."

It appears that our inquiring sister wasn't concerned with the spiritual and physical well-being of my friend, but more with the importance of setting a good example for the ward. In fact, I imagine that this sister felt that if she had to be at three hours of meetings so should everyone else.

A friend recommended the next time someone inquired about her actions, she might take them into her confidence and share with them that Heavenly Father suggested that she take the kids home, so all could get some needed rest. Now who can argue with one who seeks Heavenly Father's approval in all things?

7. Love That "Takes"

When a person serves others in order to get something in return, he is loving to "take." For example, one who teaches a Sunday School class (even though he is well prepared and teaches a beautiful lesson), then quits because all the class members are not listening or participating, is serving to "get." Or one who bakes bread for her neighbor — but only until the neighbor finds fault with her — is giving to "get." One stops going to church because the ward members are unfriendly is another example.

Another dimension of this perception is demonstrated by the sister who serves everyone at the expense of herself. That is, she serves her mother's whims, her husband's, her children's, and her neighbor's, all in order to feel accepted by them. She is using others in order to validate her feelings of self-worth. She becomes a doormat for others in order to feel accepted and needed; all of this, of course, is contrary to her spiritual worth and growth.

This type of loving others never prepares one to withstand rejection. When he is rejected by the people he serves it has a devastating effect. He feels worthless, unwanted, unloved, and he wonders where all this gospel giving has really gotten him. He feels his service is of no use; no matter how much he gives it never pays. All the giving never makes up for the rejection.

Now contrast this type of love with that which comes from Heavenly Father as one draws nearer unto him. Love from God fills one's heart with joy, and gives a desire to share that joy with others. If others reject him as he is giving to them, he is able to adjust because of his relationship with Heavenly Father. This love is real and provides the reservoir to withstand the rejection. Jesus said, "He that drinketh of the water that I shall give him shall never thirst." (John 4:14.)

Some people think that serving others means that one then is serving God, which will bring peace and joy. This is sometimes true but not always, according to my observations. The first great commandment is for one to serve God with all his heart, might, mind, and strength. And the second is like unto it, that is, to love one's neighbor as himself. (Matthew 22:36-39.) Does this mean that if I hate myself it is all right to hate my neighbor? God forbid. Does it mean that if I love myself only a little, then it is all right to love my neighbor only a little? Not so.

How, then, are we to love? The answer lies in the first commandment, to love God with all my heart. As one does this he will feel Heavenly Father's love and a sense of his great spiritual worth. Now, as one is filled with unconditional love from God and a sense of his spiritual worth, he will see the great worth in his neighbor, plus he will be filled with the kind of love that can withstand rejection. Remember that one can serve his neighbor and not serve God, but one cannot serve God without serving his neighbor.

8. The Natural Man

The natural man will not yield to the enticings of the Holy Spirit. He will not become "as a child, submissive, patient, full of love, willing to submit to all things which the Lord seeth fit to inflict upon him" because it is contrary to his nature. (Mosiah 3:19.) "The natural man receiveth not the things of the Spirit of God, for they are foolishness unto him." (Corinthians 2:14.) How does one become a natural man? By loving the things of the world more than he loves God, therefore he starts to become carnal, sensual, and devilish. (Moses 5:13.)

The natural man cannot know God, nor understand his ways, nor feel this special love and peace because he will not repent and humble himself. (Corinthians 2:11; Romans 8:6.) He becomes a law unto himself and seeks to walk in his own light.

Many times one will hear the natural man justify sin by saying that everyone should have the freedom to choose what he wants. He wants freedom of speech, even if it pollutes the spiritual nature of man. To him the spiritual nature of man does not exist. Since it is difficult to prove emperically that pornography, the degrading material on television and in magazines or at the movies, does have an effect on the spiritual nature of man, we find these activities are rolling happily along. Eventually we who are spiritual must stand up and be counted and pray that the souls of man will be touched by what we testify of and thus stay the hand of Satan. But when one testifies of the truth, the natural man will come forth to fight against him.

Have you met this kind of person? When you could not change his mind or affect his opinions, how did it make you feel? Some say, "I feel helpless, dumb, uninformed, depressed, or rejected." Satan whispers, "Jim, if you had the truth, then all would be convinced, but as you can see, few people accept what you are saying. I wonder if you really have the truth."

But we must remember that as we testify of the truth we must rely upon the Spirit to touch the heart of the listener. (2 Nephi 33:2.) If he has hardened his heart against the truth, he may not be rejecting us but the word, for he loves darkness more than light. (John 3:19.) With love in our hearts, we will prepare ourselves for his rejection. We will acknowledge that each person has two choices: to harden his heart against the truth (not us) or to come forth with a softened heart and feel the testimony by the power of the Holy Ghost. Sometimes the messenger is rejected along with the message, or he is accepted and loved. When we are rejected along with the message, we can call upon God and ask for strength and we will find peace and joy in his service. We receive great comfort from understanding the nature of man and the purpose of this earth. We have an eternal perspective of life which gives us understanding and peace as we travel the road of life and interact with the natural man.

9. Forgiving Others

To forgive others their trespasses is to become free of needing them. If one chooses to feel hurt when someone finds fault with him, it is because at that moment he does not feel the love of God. Some people admit that they get mad at what other people say or do. They know that to remain upset only hurts themselves, but they feel that they deserve to be mad for what the other person did. However, they also notice that the Spirit leaves and they are left alone if they choose not to forgive. Heavenly Father still loves them, of course, but they won't be able to feel his love because they have chosen to withdraw from the light and move into spiritual darkness.

Some people admit they were wrong in getting upset at another, but they still have difficulty getting the Holy Ghost back into their lives. They ask, "How can I get the Spirit back? I prayed and prayed but to no avail." The quickest way to get the Spirit back when it has left is to repent. That is, to go before God with a broken heart and a contrite spirit, ask for forgiveness, and seek to draw near unto him. This may mean that one asks for the other person to forgive him. You see, when one chooses to hate his brother he also chooses to hate God.

> *If a man say, I love God, and hateth his brother, he is a liar; for if he loveth not his brother whom he hath seen, how can he love God whom he hath not seen? And this commandment have we from him, that he who loveth God love his brother also.* (John 4:20-21.)

Asking God to forgive you, in and of itself, does not solve the problem. But if one follows the formula of prayer, then one will know to go to his brother and ask for forgiveness. The Savior said:

> *Wherefore, I say unto you, that ye ought to forgive one another: for he that forgiveth not his brother his trespasses standeth condemned before the Lord; for there remaineth in him the greater sin. I, the Lord, will forgive whom I will forgive, but of you it is required to forgive all men.* (D&C 64:9-10.)

Why would the greater sin be upon me, if someone committed adultery and I did not forgive him? One of the answers to that question lies in the fact that I will be judged as I judge others. (Matthew 7:2.) Therefore, if I expect others to be perfect (which is evident by the fact that I do not allow others to make any mistakes) then I will be judged according to that standard of perfection. Therefore, who will be under the greater condemnation, me or the person who sinned? I would have to conclude that it would be me. For if someone committed adultery, there is a way for him to escape if he repents and qualifies for the gift of forgiveness. But if I do not repent by forgiving him, the greater sin remaineth in me and therefore the greater condemnation. For I am judged by a standard of perfection; I have no chance of qualifying for the celestial kingdom.

I remember a young lady who had been abused by her stepfather when she was young. Her bitterness was evident and she was justified in hating her father. But the price she was paying for that hate was not worth it. She did not love herself, nor could she feel the love of her Father in Heaven. She did not trust men and her mind dwelt upon her hate constantly. She felt that if she forgave her stepfather she would be concluding that he had not wronged her. Her perception was not correct. By forgiving him she was recognizing that her hate for him was stronger than her love for God. Forgiveness could reverse these emotions. To forgive another was to admit responsibility for her negative feelings and to admit that she was wrong in allowing these feelings to remain. Why was she wrong? Because she, not the father, was paying all the consequences for her hate.

She also realized that to hate her father meant that she still needed him in order to feel good about herself. She took full responsibility for her negative feelings and turned unto Heavenly Father and asked for forgiveness. She in turn asked for her earthly father's forgiveness. Then she forgave him for his past behavior. By doing so, she felt the Holy Ghost come back into her life. She felt love from her Father in Heaven and felt love for herself as a daughter of God. She noticed how her previous hate for her father turned to sorrow. She prayed that he would repent and also receive forgiveness. She learned that she, not her father, was responsible for how she felt about herself. During the process he had not changed one bit, but she had, and now she was happy and felt the love of her Heavenly Father.

Several years ago a sister came in to see me about a personal problem. Her husband had been sick for some time and she had been the breadwinner. They were having problems paying their bills but were making progress. Then, just a week before, he had gone out and bought a television for himself, on credit, without even talking it over with her. When she got the bill, she was furious, and a fierce argument ensued. The husband then announced he was going to leave. The wife was sick about his decision. She didn't want him to leave — but she also didn't want to back down from her position.

She said, "Now, President, wasn't I justified in putting my foot down and telling him that he was in the wrong?"

"You were sure right," I said. "He had no right to spend your hard-earned money without some discussion and agreement from you. However, you also must be willing to pay the consequences for the privilege of telling him off. Which is more important to you, keeping your husband or having the joy of telling him off?"

The rule is: We find it difficult to give unconditional love to those we *need* in order to get feelings of self-worth.

What can I do when I start to feel hurt?

Turn your mind and heart to Heavenly Father. As you feel his love for you, transfer these feelings toward the person with whom you are getting upset. If your feelings for Heavenly Father are stronger than the negative feelings being produced currently, then peace and love will prevail, and you can forgive quickly. The Savior suggests "that ye ought to say in your heart — let God judge between me and thee, and reward thee according to thy deeds." (D&C 64:11.)

To hate someone would mean that I choose to allow hate to enter my being. Hate drives out love and therefore the Holy Ghost.

> *They sought evil in their hearts, and I, the Lord withheld my spirit.* (D&C 64:16.)

> *If we love one another, God dwelleth in us, and his love is perfected in*

us. Hereby know we that we dwell in him, and he in us, because he hath given us of his Spirit. (1 John 4:12–13.)

Who on the face of this earth would be so important to me that I would give up my relationship with Heavenly Father in order to hate? Who do I need so badly in order to feel good about myself that I would give up my relationship with God, when I feel rejected by that person? No one. There is not anyone whose opinion I value over my Heavenly Father's. If Heavenly Father says I am okay, as evidenced by my feeling the Holy Ghost in my life, and someone else feels that I am not okay, I will stay with my Father in Heaven's conclusions. By doing so I will be able to fulfill the commandment to love God and all men.

I personally do not know of anyone who is worth hating enough to allow me to leave the joy and happiness that is found in the strait and narrow path. You see, if someone decides to hate me and be unkind to me, and if he continues to do so, he will leave the strait and narrow path that leads to eternal life. My heart goes out to such people. If I then choose to get mad at them and stay mad, I also must leave the strait and narrow path. For me to do that I would have to give up feeling the love that my Father in Heaven has for me. I would hurt the Savior because his sacrifice would no longer be valid on my behalf. I must then pay for my sins. (D&C 19:15–18.) He feels great sorrow to see us suffer that which it is not necessary for us to suffer in order to get back into his presence. I say that no one can say or do anything to induce me to give up these great blessings.

But remember, if a person chooses to hate others and does not repent or forgive them, Heavenly Father still loves him. He may not be in a position to feel that love, but God never stops giving love. At the same time, we should not forget the consequences of not forgiving another. Do not deny the demands of justice nor the mercy (love) of God. (Alma 42:30.)

10. Forgiving Self

Some members of the Church have truly repented of their past sins, confessing them and forsaking them, but they still have not forgiven themselves. Forgiving oneself is an act of love. As one seeks for the companionship of the Holy Ghost and feels its influence, he feels peace and love. (Mosiah 4:2–3.) This means that he is forgiven by Heavenly Father. Jesus says, "I the Lord remember them [one's sins] no more." (D&C 58:42.) Hopefully, we do not choose to condemn ourselves when we sin, but only recognize the sin, accept full responsibility for it, and pay the consequences humbly. By so doing, we will find it easier to experience the joy of forgiveness. People restrict the spiritual peace that is emitted from the Holy Ghost when they don't forgive themselves. It is required of us "to forgive all men," including ourselves. (D&C 64:10.)

Why is it so hard to forgive oneself?

Because in the past we have attached our feelings of self-worth to performance. With that belief, it is hard to feel good about oneself when one's performance has been negative. But now I understand that my feelings of self-worth should be based on how Heavenly Father feels about me; and now that I have gone through the steps of repentance I can feel Heavenly Father's love. I know I have been forgiven and been made clean. I do not have to forgive myself, because I never condemned myself in the first place. I know I am back in the strait and narrow path when I feel the Holy Ghost again. Oh, what joy fills my heart! I am clean, forgiven, and acceptable to meet the Savior.

Why is it hard to some of us to confess our sins?

If my feelings of self-worth come primarily from performance or the honors of men, then there is no way I can feel good about confessing my sins. When others find out that I have made a mistake, I will have shut off the only real source of good feelings toward myself. That is, others will not respect me, admire me, or give me compliments any more. You see, with this attitude, I believe people love me for the good things I do. People do not love me because I am a son or daughter of God. If I confess my sins they will come to hate me as I hate myself. Since I love myself for performing well, I know other people love me for the same reason. No one really loves me because I am a good person who has made a mistake; that sounds too much like heaven.

All this is false, of course, as we have discussed.

Can I forgive myself of past mistakes?

Let us analyze past mistakes to discover the best way to handle them. First, everyone has made many mistakes of one kind or another. But Satan will tell us privately that "a good person would not make a mistake."

Second, our past mistakes cannot be erased, only forgiven. No matter how many tears we have shed over our mistakes, they will not go away. We can wish we had not made the mistake, we can apologize to everyone involved, we can make restitution, but the mistake or experience is still ours.

Third, there is no way to justify why we or anyone would make a mistake. There is no answer to "why" that will bring complete satisfaction to one's soul.

I remember spending three hours with a couple trying to help the wife understand why her husband had made a mistake. He had kissed their maid. We went through several scriptures like James 2:13–16, but in the final analysis I told the wife that the only thing that would bring her comfort was that he was now clean, that he was worthy to take her to the temple and preside in the home by the Spirit, that the Holy Ghost would bear her that witness and give her peace if she would also forgive him. But that could take place in her life only as she got her mind off his mistake and allowed God and Jesus Christ to determine his worthiness. She needed to humble herself until she felt the Holy Ghost in her life. Then by the Spirit she would be taught what she could do to help him. Then peace would come.

But aren't we judged by our mistakes?

We are judged by who we are, not who we were.

> *But if the wicked will turn from all his sins that he hath committed, and keep all my statutes and do that which is lawful and right, he shall surely live, he shall not die. All his transgressions that he hath committed, they shall not be mentioned unto him; in his righteousness that he hath done he shall live.* (Ezekiel 18:21-22.)

We will be judged by our present state. That is, I am judged by who I am now, with all my present feelings, faith, and acts. I will not be judged by who I used to be.

The old man of the past was buried by repentance. The new man is clean, and he desires to feed the spiritual body daily and purify the appetites, passions, and desires of the flesh to bring them under control. He loves God and Jesus Christ. He feels their love and companionship. He desires this companionship more than anything else. He is qualified for a celestial inheritance. Of course he made mistakes in the past, but God and Jesus Christ have forgotten them and will never mention them again. (D&C 58:42.) That is good enough for him. He will not commit the mistakes of the past again because he has grown spiritually. The temptations of the past are repulsive to his spiritual feelings and would not be entertained or even enticing to him.

He is thrilled and overjoyed in this life because he is clean, not because he is perfect or because he has never made a mistake.

How can one feel good about his past mistakes?

When one's emotions are very deep, and are intensified by embarrassment and remorse from sinning, he will not feel good about his mistakes. It takes time to rebuild good spiritual feelings about oneself. When one's spiritually based feelings about Heavenly Father and Jesus Christ become greater than the feelings created from the mistake, he will be overjoyed. He will stop judging himself and will base his feelings of worth on revelation and his spiritual worth. He will feel Heavenly Father's love for him, and as he builds these spiritual feelings daily in his life, he will find that his past mistakes will have little effect on him.

Remember, it takes time to build a spiritual reservoir after one has emptied it. One should give himself time to rebuild his spiritual feelings. The end result is well worth the effort and time required.

Be Patient with Self

Remember that one's dominating emotions determine his actions; therefore, when one makes a mistake he must be patient with himself.

Suppose, for example, you are leaving a church meeting and returning to your new car, parked just outside. As you reach your car, you are shocked to see that someone has just rammed into its side. You could react in one of three ways. First, you could go up to the person and hit him in the nose for being so careless. Or you could restrain your fists and just verbally attack the person. Or you could ask him the Golden Questions. What you do will be based upon your dominating emotions at that moment.

This situation of someone hitting your car creates certain feelings. If these feelings are greater than your present feelings for the Savior, then you will probably hit or verbally attack the person. However, as the day goes by, the feelings created by the accident will become weaker. Sooner or later these feelings will become less dominant than the feelings you have for the Savior. When that happens, you will feed bad about what you said or did. You will ask yourself, "Why do I do such dumb things when I know better?" However, you may prolong these emotions by talking to others about how dumb this fellow was and all the problems he has created for you. But eventually these emotions will be weakened and the feelings for the Savior will become dominant.

The only way I know that a person can stop losing control

when various problems occur is to develop stronger feelings for Heavenly Father. That is, as one feels after Heavenly Father each day, eventually these feelings will become so dominant that all other feelings will be subservient. Then, when someone hits his car or puts him down, he will immediately call on God to help him through the situation. He will desire to handle each situation as Heavenly Father would want him to: with unconditional love. Each experience will therefore bring joy and happiness to him and others.

However, until we reach that point, we must not let Satan put us down when we act in an un-Christian way. We should keep progressing, be patient with ourselves and forgive ourselves and someday we will reach that point of full control. But we cannot expect to act perfectly until we have paid the price in full spirituality.

11. Expressing One's Feelings Verbally

Some people feel that if they do not verbally express their feelings no one will be hurt. The truth is that one's feelings are expressed to others even if nothing is said; others know when someone is upset or happy or depressed. One problem that arises when one fails to verbalize his feelings is that others may assume they were the cause of the problem or they may misinterpret what the other person really is feeling. Another problem is that one can become a doormat for others, all in the name of not wanting to say anything and hurt their feelings.

For one to verbalize his feelings is to initiate an act of love. Walls develop between loved ones when true feelings are not verbalized. Expressing one's true feelings verbally will not cause hurt feelings in others, if they are expressed correctly. Doing so will help build close relationships between loved ones and create a happy environment to live in.

What is a good approach to expressing our true feelings?

First, one needs to take ownership of his feelings and not disown by blaming others for making him feel a certain way. For example, when one takes ownership for how he feels he will use "I" statements: "**I** feel frustrated; **I** am upset at what is happening here; or **I** dislike these kinds of movies." When one is disowning, he makes "You" statements: "**You** make me so mad; **you** scare me when **you** drive that way; or **you** always spend over the budget." "You" statements are fault-finding, accusatory, and place the blame on someone else. The result of "You" statements is to put others on the defense; they in turn find fault with the person who makes the statements.

Like attracts like. When one finds fault with another, normally he will get fault-finding in return.

Second, the focus must be on expressing your *real* feelings, so others will know how you feel. The focus *is not* on the relationship. For example, a wife is frustrated at her husband for inviting people home to dinner without asking for her approval. She will express her feelings even if he chooses to get upset. That is his problem and only he can solve it. She may say, "Frank, I love you and desire to help you any way I can, but I feel very frustrated and used when people are invited to our home, and I am expected to feed them, and no one checks to see if my schedule will permit it. I realize this is my problem, not yours, but I want you to know that I will not serve any more guests if you haven't sought my approval before they are invited. If you want to clean the house, cook the meal, and clean up afterwards, I want you to know that I will not be offended. Do you understand how I feel?"

Now the husband may get upset and put her down; he may explain her duties to her as his wife; but she will not participate in that discussion, except to acknowledge that she can see that he is upset. *Her focus and only goal is to express her feelings,* so he will understand how she feels. Her goal is not to put him down, or plead "poor me," or get him to solve her problem. She realizes she must pay a price for expressing her feelings, but it is worth it, for in the long run the marriage will become stronger.

Third, before one expresses his feelings to another, he needs to be sensitive to the Spirit. That is, one would not choose a time when the other person is depressed or overly tired, or when others are around. One would express these feelings as if the Savior were present. He would prayerfully ask for help so that all may benefit as he expresses his feelings. And the receiver would perceive these feelings of love expressed in voice tones, posture, timing, and what is being said.

12. Dumping from Others

What can a person do when someone else is dumping verbally on him — that is, they use "You" statements blaming him for how they feel?

First, quickly recognize that the other person is disowning and trying to get you to be responsible for how he feels.

Second, turn the focus onto the accuser and how he feels, rather than on the one being dumped on. For example, "John, **you** make me so mad. **Your** driving is reckless, and **you** couldn't care less about the laws of this land. My sixteen-year-old drives better than **you** do."

Now, John could find fault with Steve by telling him to shut up — after all, Steve's driving isn't that great either. But John recognizes the dumping taking place so he concentrates on what Steve is feeling. "Steve, I am sorry if my driving is frustrating you. I can sense that this is really upsetting to you."

Now, Steve may continue to find fault, but John continues to focus on what he perceives as Steve's feelings and frustration. John may even slow down, trying to be sensitive to Steve's feelings, but John doesn't take any blame or responsibility for Steve's frustrations.

But, you say, maybe John's driving *is* reckless and frightening, and someone needs to let John know. That may be true, but not to the point of blaming (dumping on) John for how the other person feels.

Steve could have said, "John, I really get upset when we go around corners that fast; it appears dangerous to me and I fear I could get killed. I know this may be silly to you, but I would appreciate it if you would slow down."

"Steve, you sure are a chicken if this scares you."

"You may be right, John, but if you aren't going to slow down, please let me out at the next corner. Thanks!"

Here, Steve recognized he had the problem and solved it. No longer was he dumping and trying to pass on responsibility for his problem.

Section V

FEELING COMPLETELY FORGIVEN FOR PAST SINS

Many people who walk in the strait and narrow path feel like they haven't been completely forgiven of their past sins and mistakes. They know they have repented, for they have felt the sorrow, have suffered the pains for sin, have confessed, made restitution, and are active in the Kingdom of God. Because of repentance they have felt the love of God come back into their lives, they have seen relationships with others repaired, and they have been called by God to serve in the Church. But for some reason they have a deep feeling inside of themselves that all is not well, that there is something else they need to do. It is a feeling of unworthiness, like they will never feel worthy to meet the Savior because they made a mistake in the past. When they made the mistake, they knew it was wrong, but they never realized the magnitude of the price they would have to pay. Deep down they feel that if others knew of their past mistakes, those others wouldn't respect them as highly as they do now. These feelings create an atmosphere of uneasiness and fear, rather than openness, acceptance, and feelings of love.

The purpose of this section is to outline the effects of walking in spiritual darkness and indicate how to overcome these effects as one walks in the strait and narrow path. As one applies the principles taught in this section, he will come to know that he has been forgiven of his past sins. He will feel worthy to meet the Savior; his desire to serve God will increase; and his past mistakes will have little effect on how others feel about him. His faith in God, self, and others will increase. And most of all, he will feel peace in this life and an increase of hope in his qualifying for eternal life. (Remember how important hope is!) How will all this be possible? Because he will come to know the truth, and the truth can make him free from past mistakes and Satan's influence.

Chapter Twelve

Overcoming the Effects of Walking in Spiritual Darkness

To MAKE SURE WE ARE all on the same wavelength, let's begin with some definitions:

Spiritual Darkness: To walk without the Spirit of God.

Spiritual Light: To walk with the Spirit of God and receive revelation.

Sin: To transgress the laws of God according to one's light and knowledge.

The Effects of Walking in Spiritual Darkness

And what are the effects of walking in spiritual darkness? Here are several I've observed in many different individuals, including myself:

Mistrust: Many individuals have witnessed that trusting relationships deteriorate after committing a sin. They still feel a need to be trusted by others, but the trust is not to be found.

Trust from others is a basic ingredient to success. It takes years to build a trusting relationship. And since that trust must be earned, it is not a gift; and a few untrustworthy actions can negate years of building a trusting relationship. The sad part of this scenario is that if one chooses to continue to walk in spiritual darkness, these special relationships will never be experienced again.

Why is not trust a gift? Why must it be earned?

It takes effort, time, and experience to develop the reputation of a trusted individual. For example, when parents reject their teenager's request to drive the car during bad weather, he may respond,"You don't trust me!" But the teenage son lacks experience in driving a car in bad weather. Trust is not even a consideration in this example. How can parents trust their son in a situation he has never experienced or prepared for in advance. The parents know that it is unwise to let their son drive in conditions that could lead to an accident with serious and long-lasting consequences. The reasons or need to drive the car that night are nothing compared to the possible consequences.

Unlike trust, however, love is a gift that does not have to be earned or bought. It is free, from Heavenly Father as well as from earthly parents, as one prepares himself to receive it. The parents declined the son's request to drive the car in bad weather because they love him.

Closeness: Those who choose to commit adultery or to lie and cheat others, and do not repent of these sins, experience the loss of spiritual closeness to spouse, children, friends, Heavenly Father, and themselves. They feel a deficiency within themselves for the lack of shared feelings of love, tenderness, kindness, joy, and peace. These kinds of deep, positive feelings can be experienced only in their spiritual dimension, which has been cut off from their awareness. They are left alone to suffer the pain that comes to all who choose to walk in spiritual darkness.

Such people will try to overcome these deficiencies through the physical appetites, passions, and desires. The result of such choices of course, can only be a greater deficiency.

Over-stimulations of appetites, passions, and desires: Those who walk in spiritual darkness find that the appetites, passions, and desires of the flesh soon become over-stimulated. These appetites then consume the energy of their minds, emotions, and strengths. At times, they are so driven to meet these demands that it seems as if they are not in control. These desires can be satisfied only temporarily, however. The person feels something of worth missing from his life. He feels great needs but cannot fill them.

Below are listed some of the appetites, passions, and desires of the flesh and of the world. (see Galatians 5:16–26.)

1. Vain glory
2. Envying one another
3. Provoking one another
4. Anger/hatred
5. Overeating
6. Overspending
7. Impatience
8. Carnal desires
   a. Adultery/fornication
   b. Petting
   c. Pornography
   d. R- and X-rated movies
   e. Masturbation
   f. Homosexuality
9. Murder
10. Drunkenness
11. Material possessions for personal worth
12. Gambling
13. Being unforgiving
14. Hardening one's heart against the spirit

One may either open his heart to spiritual things and feel after them, or he may harden his heart against the Spirit of God. That is, he may close his emotions toward something, or he may open his heart and feel after something. The opposite of a hardened heart is a broken heart. One who has a broken heart and contrite spirit is one who is able to feel and understand when the Spirit of God speaks. To have a broken heart is to have an open heart toward spiritual things, one that can feel and be emotionally involved.

Someone who has hardened his heart against the Spirit of God has developed the attitude that experiences of a spiritual nature are foolishness. (1 Corinthians 2:14.) He has no desire to feel after the Spirit of God. He will not prepare himself to receive revelation; that is, he will not keep the commandments or pray or exercise faith. (1 Nephi 15:8-11.)

One can close his heart to sin, pornography, lying, cheating, stealing, and so forth, or he can open his heart to such things. As he opens his heart to such vices, he overstimulates the appetites, passions, and desires of the flesh and kills the feelings of the Spirit. And as he overstimulates these appetites of the flesh, the flesh demands more and more in order to be satisfied. Eventually a person can reach a state where he is "past feeling." That is, he can kill the spiritual feeling inside to the degree that he can no longer feel the promptings of the Spirit. In the end, he will no longer feel the Spirit of God, his feelings for loved ones will be deadened, and, saddest of all, he will reach the point where he is "past" feeling love for himself as a child of God.

Since dominating emotions determine actions, whenever one overstimulates the appetites, passions, and desires of the flesh it becomes very hard to concentrate on spiritual things. He continually feels drawn back toward the sin, even though he doesn't want to return unto the sin.

Feelings of self-worth — ZERO

The longer one walks in spiritual darkness, the closer he comes to feeling that he is nothing. The longer he is in spiritual darkness, the more he will feel inadequate, unimportant, incapable, and unloved. He will come to feel worthless. He will feel uncomfortable around other members of the Church. In fact, many members feel embarrassed and uncomfortable while attending church. They agree that the members are friendly and make a sincere effort to help them feel welcome, but they still feel uneasy.

Those who are walking in spiritual darkness feel rejected. When negative comments are made about them, they feel devastated in their feelings of self-worth. They spend most of their lives seeking to prove their personal worth. They operate under conditional love. They have a hard time feeling their spiritual worth or that of others. The longer they walk in spiritual darkness the more they have to rely on other sources to feel of any value.

Externals will control

Feelings of self-worth for the spiritually deprived come from material possessions, honors of men, and performance. (D&C 121:34, 35.) If one has a new Cadillac, new clothes, a large bank account or a great deal of real estate, then he will feel good about himself. That is, he will feel that he is worth something. He will feel good about what he has accomplished and, therefore, he can feel good about himself. He will feel that he is better than others because he has accomplished more than others. Since others look up to him for his great performance or accomplishments, he feels accepted by others. On the other hand, of course, if he did not have much money or good clothes, he would feel inferior and of little worth compared to those who have achieved greater material possessions.

Our spiritually deprived person feels good about himself when others express good feelings about him. If others do not like him or if they express negative feelings about the way he looks or expresses himself, then our friend feels negative about himself. This type of experience creates a climate where he feels inferior to others—thus his need to be accepted by the world increases. Many times he feels the Church interferes with his life, since the Church rejects most of the acceptable standards of the world.

Performance or accomplishment has a great influence on this

person's feelings of self-worth. That is, he feels great about himself if he gets As or Bs in school. If he gets Ds or Fs he does not feel good about himself. If he gets more sales than his friend, he feels good about himself; but if he is last in sales he feels worthless. If his kids are in trouble at school or not living the commandments, he feels unworthy. He feels he has failed and, therefore, is not worthy to enter the celestial kingdom. If his children are performing well in sports, in the band, or at church, he feels great about himself. He has mixed up his performance with his worth.

You see, when one is spiritually weak, externals are taken personally. If the externals are positive he will rejoice. If they are negative he will become angered. "For his house is built upon sand and when the rains descend, and the floods come, and the winds blow, and beat upon that house. . . . " (Matthew 7:26-27.)

When one walks in spiritual darkness, he sees all things as an extension of himself. The negatives of the world are taken personally and then magnified.

A spiritually dominant person sees externals as externals. He sees others' personal problems as their problems. If his children have problems, he sees those problems as the children's problems and does not take them personally. Since he cares about his children, he may be very hurt over their actions and decisions, but rather than becoming angered he will turn to Heavenly Father for comfort and direction.

Removes faith/hope (creates mud puddle)

In order for faith to be faith it must be centered in God. The person who walks in spiritual darkness will be guided only by the spirit of man which is in him. (1 Corinthians 2:11.) He therefore is limited in his ability to move forward, because he cannot see clearly. He does not know of that which would be of most worth to him. He has many fears and worries, since ill health or death could be around the next corner. He has no hope in the resurrection of Jesus Christ or in Christ's ability to raise him from the grave. He must take whatever he can for himself today, for tomorrow may be his time to die.

Those who have walked in spiritual darkness for years have found that the consequences of their many mistakes have accumulated. These consequences have created an environment that seems to have completely taken control of their life. The faith and hope necessary to overcome these burdens are lacking; therefore, the effort needed to improve their present circumstances is completely absent. The only thing they can do is to complain about their circumstances and how hopeless they feel. They take no responsibility for the harvest of the seeds they have sown previously. And they seem to be executing solutions (so-called) that will eventually bring even greater tragedy into their lives. We call this condition the "mud puddle" problem.

As a young bishop, I used to spend hours trying to get people out of the mud puddle. My success in this method was near zero, and over the years I wondered why. Then I learned a great lesson which has helped me both save time and touch people's lives.

Mud Puddle Theory

Picture in your mind someone sitting in the middle of a large mud puddle which is cold, muddy, and dirty. They complain how cold the water is and how awful it is to be in such dirty circumstances. They complain of uncaring husbands or money difficulties or problems with their bosses or jobs. They never take responsibility for their problems; they never make any determination to overcome or endure.

I used to encourage such people to come out of the water, but they would tell me it was no use. "I couldn't get out even if I tried," they would say. I would extend my hand and promise them that if they would grab hold, I could help pull them out. But they kept their arms folded and said, "That positive mental attitude stuff doesn't work. I've tried it before, and it did not work then so it could not work now."

I pleaded and pleaded, quoted scriptures, read the words of the prophets, held fasts in their behalf, and all to no avail. They had no hope and would no longer try. All they would do was complain about the cold, muddy, and dirty water. They would sob and ask for help; they would explain how much they longed to get out of that condition — but still they made no effort to escape.

Then I learned why, and it was pure revelation to me. The thought was expressed by Albert E. N. Gray in a talk called the "Common Denominator of Success."[1] He explained, in essence, that it is easier for people to adjust to the cold, dirty, muddy water than it is to adjust to the hardships of paying the price to get out.

The law of free agency allows each person the right to choose which laws he will keep and which he will reject. Bishops, home teachers, visiting teachers, and others can listen to those who want to stay in the cold, muddy, dirty water. They can cry with them, comfort them, visit them, and be understanding. But those in the puddle will experience little improvement until they choose to repent and accept responsibility for their mistakes and expend the energy necessary to bring peace and happiness into their lives.

Now when I see people in the mud puddle, I still feel sorry for them, but I understand why they do not let others help them get out. They feel it is easier to stay in.

Doubts develop

Since heaven cannot reach a person who is in spiritual darkness — because darkness cannot comprehend spiritual light (John 1:5) — he can very easily be influenced by Satan's lies. Doubts become all-consuming in his mind. He learns to doubt his worth, his purposes, even his ability to succeed, and even his God. Worry, frustration, anxieties, guilt feelings, and fears are born and developed as one lives in spiritual darkness.

---

1. Albert E. N. Gray, "Common Denominator of Success," National Association of Life Underwriters, Washington, D.C., reprinted Aug. 1976.

When one walks in spiritual darkness he is "tossed to and fro, and carried about with every wind of doctrine." (Ephesians 4:14.) Satan teaches him the wrong formula for success. He teaches him not to trust others. Love others if they do what you say. Love your children if they make you proud. Let your children make up their own minds about right and wrong. Sacrifice for others is ridiculous. The stimulation of carnal desires is natural and acceptable. Confessing your sins is childish. A life of ease brings happiness. God loves you only when you do right. You must be perfect to inherit the celestial kingdom. You are acceptable to God only when you perform well. Your worth is determined by how many commandments you keep. And on and on and on. Satan is the father of all lies and he is a master of his trade.

Other Effects of Walking in Spiritual Darkness:

No spiritual growth	No hope in eternal life
A need to be perfect	No peace, joy, love
No hope in the future	Must atone for own sins
No revelation	No eternal families
State of despair	Eternal progression limited
Health problems	Telestial view of this life
Double-minded	Fears
Contention	Anger/hate
Wars	Jealousy/envy
Selfishness	Loss of feelings of spiritual worth

Wages — Who is responsible for the consequences of sin?

Alma tells us that "every man receiveth wages of him whom he listeth to obey." (Alma 3:27.) Some of the wages of sin have been listed above — but the greatest of those wages is death, spiritual death. No one can walk in spiritual darkness and not suffer the consequences, for they are automatic. The demands of justice invariably see to it that we suffer the consequences of our actions. On the other hand, the blessings are automatic when we are obedient to a law.

Helaman reviewed these ideas as follows:

> *Whosoever perisheth, perisheth unto himself; and whosoever doeth iniquity, doeth it unto himself; for behold, ye are free; ye are permitted to act for yourselves; for behold, God hath given unto you a knowledge and he hath made you free . . . and ye can do good and be restored unto that which is good, or have that which is good restored unto you; or ye can do evil, and have that which is evil restored unto you.* (Helaman 14:30, 31.)

I have heard some leaders indicate that they have difficulty counseling people about sin over the pulpit. They say that one can be forgiven of committing adultery, but how does one teach this in a public meeting? It appears to me that those who commit adultery can be forgiven of their sin but the demands of justice will see to it that the consequences will follow, and these consequences may take years to overcome.

I know a man who was excommunicated from the Church for adultery and was working his way back into the strait and narrow path. However, he had to be on guard when beautiful women passed by, for he had to shift his mind and heart from the present moment unto Heavenly Father so he would not have tempting thoughts that would arouse the flesh.

James talked about this process as follows:

> *Let no man say when he is tempted, I am tempted of God: for God cannot be tempted with evil, neither tempteth he any man. But every man is tempted, when he is drawn away of his own lust, and enticed. Then when lust hath conceived, it bringeth forth sin . . . and sin, when it is finished, bringeth forth death.* (James 1:13–15.)

Those who are called to teach need to explain the consequences of sin, which can follow one even after he has been forgiven.

How does one get into spiritual darkness?

From the strait and narrow path, one can sin and not desire to repent. That is, they come to love spiritual darkness more than walking in the light. By doing so they leave the path and enter into spiritual darkness and no longer have the companionship of the Holy Ghost. They thereby close the heavens against themselves. For some, it is easier to endure the wages of sin than to suffer the embarrassment of confessing and allowing others to learn of their mistake. They therefore choose to remain in spiritual darkness.

One can get into spiritual darkness by neglect. That is, in order to stay in the strait and narrow path, one must press forward; (2 Nephi 31:20.) then the light will grow brighter and brighter until he gains a fullness. (D&C 50:24.) A person cannot be associated with the Godhead daily and not improve in light and truth. If he loses his desire to walk in the light and to improve, though, eventually he will come to love darkness more than light and will be found in darkness. (D&C 84:54.) This sometimes comes about because he gives up hope that he will ever qualify for eternal life.

Traditions taught in the world can limit the growth of one's light. All of us have been taught untruths in our homes and schools, by peer groups and society. The problem is that we do not know that many of these teachings are not true, that they are lies. As long as we do not recognize these untruths they will continue to limit our spiritual growth.

For example, we were taught in school that if one gets "A"s he is a good person and acceptable. If he gets "F"s he is not acceptable. Our parents many times showed their love to us when we did what was right. When we did what was wrong they did not show love, and we felt unacceptable. We therefore felt we had to prove our worth to them.

Another untruth people are taught is that performance determines our worth. Or that the person with the most money or wealth is the most successful. He may lose his wife and family in the process but if he has a lot of money, he must be okay. Another example: one's success is based upon what other people think, rather than on what one thinks of himself. And another: I am responsible for other people's feelings.

Some will use guilt feelings to condemn themselves, thereby putting themselves deeper into spiritual darkness. They fail to realize that such feelings are signals from God telling us to repent and turn unto him.

Those outside the Church are in spiritual darkness because of their sins. Nonmembers can be forgiven if they will hearken unto the Spirit of Christ. They will then receive light and truth, (D&C 84:45-53.) teaching them to have faith, repent, and be baptized. But if they decide to continue to walk by their own light, they will find themselves in spiritual darkness. (Helaman 12:6.)

But when I am in the strait and narrow path, why don't I always feel at peace, forgiven, and free from struggle?

CONCEPT NUMBER ONE
Satan wants a person to continually feel bad about the sin, while Heavenly Father wants him to feel bad about losing the companionship of the Holy Ghost.

Suppose, for example, a person commits the sin of adultery. The Spirit withdraws, and he experiences guilt feelings. He knows he is wrong; he has offended God, his wife, and his family. He feels sick inside; everything that has been important to him has been thrown away for a brief moment of excitement.

Now Satan moves in and helps the person along the road to despair. He points out the embarrassment that will follow if the person chooses to confess the sin. He suggests that there is no value in repenting, for a sinner is not going to make it to the celestial kingdom anyway. He then starts the "Remember when?" series. It goes something like this:

"Jim, I really feel bad that you have fallen again. It looks like this time you really blew it. Now, while I have your attention let me review your past mistakes, so you can really see the complete picture and how hopeless your situation is. Remember when you stole that item? I told you then that you would never make it. And remember when . . . ?"

Satan then helps the person remember all his past sins, all two hundred of them. What is the end result? The person feels no good, worthless, unloved, incapable, discouraged, and he concludes, why even try — I will never make it anyway. But don't forget — Satan is a liar.

The Savior's way will bring peace and hope, and it will create an environment where one can feel the love of God again. When one sins, the Spirit withdraws and guilt feelings of wrong doing set in. But rather than listening to Satan's lies, the person chooses to turn to God because he feels bad about losing the companionship of the Holy Ghost. *His focus is on losing the Spirit and not on the mistake.*

How does one get the Holy Ghost back into his life? By repenting, by seeking God's forgiveness, by feeling God's love, and by believing that he will be forgiven as he seeks with all his heart to qualify for the gift again.

With his mind and heart focused upon God and Jesus Christ, knowing that he is loved and wanted back into the strait and narrow path, he is ready to see the consequences of his acts. What price is too great to pay to be reconciled unto God and Jesus Christ? If one has to confess to a spouse, the children, the bishop, and the ward, if one has to be excommunicated and suffer great embarrassment in order to come back into the arms of God and the Savior, it is all worth it. And as he **focuses** on the reward of feeling God's love and forgiveness, the price he has to pay for the sin is well worth it. But if he **focuses** only on the sin and the consequences of sin as he repents, as Satan wants him to do, despair and discouragement set in. Why? Because Satan is discounting the saving principle of faith. In order for one to repent, he needs to **exercise faith** in God, the Savior, and in the principle of forgiveness. *And the key to exercising faith is to be able to see the fruits of one's labor before they are earned.*

Alma reviews this principle as follows:

> *But if ye will nourish the word, yea, nourish the tree as it beginneth*
> *to grow, by your faith with great diligence, and with patience, looking*
> *forward to the fruit thereof, it shall take root."* (Alma 32:41.)

If a person focuses on housework while never seeing the goal of having a clean house, or on temple work while never seeing the joy of those whose work is being performed, the weight of the effort becomes more than he or she can bear. To labor with teenagers while never feeling that each child will make it produces despair, not faith and energy. But he who sees the fruits of his labors before they are accomplished is able to exercise faith sufficient to endure until the harvest is ready. There is no other way we can have such endurance.

If a person has repented of his sins and is now walking in the strait and narrow path, yet still doesn't always feel forgiven, could it be caused by his *focusing on the mistake,* which allows Satan to move in for a discussion? If our friend will observe what is happening as he chooses to *focus on his past mistakes,* he will become aware that the Holy Ghost is withdrawing. But when he *focuses on serving Heavenly Father,* he will observe that the Spirit remains, even when his past mistakes enter his mind. This will occur when he no longer chooses to play Satan's game of "remember when . . . ?" He knows he has sinned in the past, but he will not waste the present moment by discussing the past with Satan. Instead he chooses to concentrate on bringing forth fruit meet for repentance by concentrating on walking by the Spirit.

> *Behold, he who has repented of his sins, the same is forgiven, and I,*
> *the Lord, remember them no more.* (D&C 58:42.)

If Christ doesn't remember our past sins, who is it that brings them back to our remembrance? Satan. When past sins come into our mind, then, we can know Satan wants a discussion; and we can immediately recognize what is happening. We can tell Satan to go jump in the lake — and then turn our minds and hearts to God and seek to serve him.

CONCEPT NUMBER TWO
**The effects of sinning accompany
a person into the strait and narrow path,
even though he has fully repented.**

In the example above, our friend had committed adultery. Consider some prices he will have to pay as a result of this sin:

1. His spouse will mistrust him in the future.
2. He will lose a certain amount of closeness to his wife.
3. He will struggle with overstimulation of the flesh. In the future, he may be tempted by the worldly display of sex.
4. His spiritual feeling of self-worth will diminish and become very low.
5. He will begin to be controlled by externals, such as how others feel about him.
6. His ability to exercise faith will be low.
7. Doubts about himself and spiritual things will grow to high levels.

Let us assume our friend has repented and now is walking in the strait and narrow path. Does this mean that his wife and children now fully trust him and feel a closeness to him? Will repentance automatically restore his feelings of self-worth and his faith? Will it remove all doubts from his mind? Does repentance mean that he will not be tempted when sexual displays are shown on television? The answer to all these questions is **nay.** It may take years for our friend to rebuild the bridge of trust with his family and to develop spiritual closeness with his wife.

When one repents and qualifies to enter the strait and narrow path, he thereby is forgiven, but that doesn't mean the effects of his sin are all washed away. What repentance does is put one in a position to feel the Holy Ghost, which creates an atmosphere in which we can feel the **love** of Heavenly Father. No one can overcome the effects of sin without feeling the love of God in abundance to sustain him as he makes restitution. As one walks

through life feeling the love of God and the guidance of the Holy
Ghost, he will one day become aware that he has been sanctified
from his past sin. He no longer will be tempted by sexual displays;
in fact, he will be repulsed by them. He now feels a spiritual
closeness to his wife and family. His feelings of self-worth have
grown, and he no longer is dependent upon others for his feelings
of self-worth.

Some people have falsely concluded that since they are still
struggling with their spouses, and since they still feel temptation
at times, they must not be forgiven. They have failed to realize
that it takes time to overcome the effects of spiritual darkness,
though with God's help one **can** eventually overcome.

This is reviewed and clarified by Alma to his son Corianton.
Corianton had committed a serious sin while he was on a mission
to the Zoramites. Alma worked with his son, carefully explaining
the gospel in chapters 39-42 of the Book of Alma. He concluded
the instruction as follows:

> *O my son, I desire that ye should deny the justice of God no more. Do*
> *not endeavor to excuse yourself in the least point because of your sins, by*
> *denying the justice of God. . . .*

Note: In other words, do not feel that God doesn't love a person
because that person must suffer the effects of walking in spiritual
darkness, for the justice department sees to it that all of us
experience the immediate effects of our sins — even though
Christ will remove the eternal consequences of those sins for the
repentant. We ought therefore to avoid choosing to get upset
because we must take responsibility for our own mistakes. God
doesn't remove the effects of one's mistakes, but he does support
a person as he overcomes the effects.

> *. . . but do let the justice of God and his mercy, and his long-*
> *suffering have full sway in your heart, and let it bring you down to the*
> *dust in humility.* (Alma 42:30.)

Note: What should have full sway in one's heart? The justice of
God (which allows and sometimes administers the effects of

walking in spiritual darkness) and God's mercy and longsuffering (feeling in abundance the love God has for him).

After his sin and repentance our friend will therefore recognize that his wife is still struggling with trusting him. He will say in his heart, "I know, Father, that my wife is struggling with me. I recognize that this is caused by my sin. Help me to show love and patience until she can fully trust me again. I know thou lovest me and hast fully forgiven me and now thou art with me daily, sustaining me as I meet the demands of justice and overcome the effects of walking in spiritual darkness, for without thee I could not endure."

CONCEPT NUMBER THREE
It is hard to feel forgiven of one's sins if one's sense of worth is tied to performance.

If a person's feelings of self-worth come primarily from his performance and from the opinions of others, then when he sins he feels of little worth. Therefore, when his past sins come into his mind he will feel worthless and not forgiven. Why? Because he values the assessment of man over that of God, which puts him, at least to a degree, in spiritual darkness, where he cannot feel the companionship of the Spirit.

But the friend we have been discussing has now built his feelings of self-worth upon his value to Heavenly Father. He knows that God never stops loving him. When past mistakes come into his mind he recognizes that Satan is trying to get him to concentrate on his past so he will become discouraged. Instead, our friend chooses to pray and seek the guidance of Heavenly Father. He seeks to work on his spiritual growth and refuses to play Satan's game of condemning himself because of past mistakes. He knows that God will judge him on *who* he is now and *what* he is doing now, and not on what he did in the past.

> *But if the wicked will turn from all his sins that he hath committed and keep all my statutes, and do that which is lawful and right, he shall*

surely live, he shall not die. All his transgressions that he hath committed, they shall not be mentioned unto him: in his righteousness that he hath done he shall live. (Ezekiel 18:21–22.)

CONCEPT NUMBER FOUR
Godly sorrow only, and not worldly sorrow, can overcome the emotional drain of past sins.

Dominating emotions determine one's actions. If a person's feelings for Heavenly Father and Jesus Christ are stronger and deeper than the emotional pull from past sins, then one has overcome. When someone has sinned he is usually counseled to stay away from people and places that could be tempting. Why such counsel? Because once a person has overstimulated the appetites, passions, and desires of the flesh, it takes great effort for him to develop emotions that will be stronger than those developed in sinning. If he chooses to enter those places that are designed to stimulate the appetites of the flesh, the Spirit withdraws and he is left alone to fight the world. And alone he will lose.

How does one develop his spiritual emotions so they are dominant over the appetites of the flesh, especially after he has sinned? Included in the steps of repentance is the process of going through godly sorrow. Worldly sorrow will never produce emotions strong enough to help us overcome the appetites of the flesh. Worldly sorrow comes when a person is embarrassed at being discovered. He may cry because of this exposure and the suffering his family may have to endure. He hurts because he knows that others will know the truth and he loves darkness (secrecy) rather than light (confessing). This type of sorrow will never cleanse a person from the effects of sin; all it will do is motivate him to be more careful next time so he will not get caught.

Godly sorrow is an emotional experience designed to create the kind of dominating emotions that will help a person draw unto

God rather than the desires and pleasures of the world. President Kimball reviews this necessary emotional experience:

> Do you think you should pay no price? no penalty? no adjustments? Analyze it. Do you think you yourselves would be better off if you went free? . . . *there must be a washing, a purging, a change of attitudes, a correcting of appraisals, a strengthening toward selfmastery.* And these cleansing processes cannot be accomplished as easily as taking a bath or shampooing the hair, or sending a suit of clothes to the cleaners. *There must be many prayers, and volumes of tears.* There must be more than a verbal acknowledgement. There must be an *inner conviction* giving to the sin its full diabolical weight. "My sins are disgusting, loathsome." One could come to think about his baser sins like the Psalmist who used these words: **"My wounds stink and are corrupt because of my foolishness."** (Psalms 38:5.) There must be *increased devotion* and much *thought* and *study.* There must be a *re-awakening, a fortification, a re-birth.* And this takes energy and time and often is accompanied with *sore embarrassment, heavy deprivations and deep trials,* even if indeed one is not excommunicated from the Church, losing all spiritual blessings. [2]

The focus in this emotional experience is on the Savior and his sacrifice. As one feels the love of the Savior for him, the suffering in the garden, the bleeding from every pore on his behalf, one promises never to do it again. Through these experiences a person develops a special love for God and Christ which is desirable and brings peace. He works to maintain these feelings, and he chooses not to go where he could be tempted and lose the influence of the Spirit. He knows it will take years to develop the deep spiritual feelings necessary to withstand the temptations of the world, so he seeks for situations where he can grow spiritually. The greater the emotional experience in repenting,

---

2. Spencer W. Kimball, *Miracle of Forgiveness,* p. 155.

the easier it is to maintain the spiritual feelings and not be influenced by temptations.

CONCEPT NUMBER FIVE
One knows he has been forgiven of past sins as he feels the Holy Ghost in his life.

When a person feels the influence of the Holy Ghost in his life he knows several things about his relationship to God and the spiritual dimension:

1. He knows he is clean (forgiven of his sins).
2. He knows he is in the strait and narrow path, qualified for the celestial kingdom today.
3. He knows that, according to Heavenly Father, he is spiritually all right, worthy to serve.
4. He knows that as he prays he is eligible to receive revelation; therefore, he has no reason to doubt.
5. He knows he is progressing.

If God feels I am forgiven, this is good enough for me. I will choose to run these feelings through my mind and heart rather than reviewing how bad I was because of past mistakes.

Can one completely overcome all temptation in this life?

Brigham Young answered this question:

Do not suppose that we shall ever in the flesh be free from temptations to sin. Some suppose that they can in the flesh be sanctified in body and spirit and become so pure that they will never again feel the effects of the power of the adversary of truth. Were it possible for a person to attain to this degree of perfection in the flesh, he could not die, neither remain in a world where sin predominates. Sin has entered into the world, and death by sin. (Romans 5:12.) I think we shall more or less feel the effects of sin so long as we live, and finally have to pass the ordeals of death.... We should so live as to make the world and all its natural blessings subservient to our reasonable wants and holy desires. [3]

How can I feel the Holy Ghost in my life?

Many members have asked, "How can you tell that you have the companionship of the Holy Ghost each day?" Let's consider three ways:

1. Prayer

When we pray we don't always feel the Holy Ghost. Sometimes his influence is strong; sometimes it is very weak. I wonder sometimes if we would really be tested if the Holy Ghost's influence were so strong every day of our lives. What if we felt the influence of the Spirit so strongly that we could hear the Tabernacle Choir singing overhead when we did right — and then the sounds of the choir grew faint when we moved in the wrong direction? In that kind of setting, would we really grow in our faith?

I have had General Authorities in my home, and they have said that the power of the Holy Ghost varies in their lives. Sometimes the influence is very strong and other times very weak. Many times these brethren are left to walk by the light they have developed thus far, but they always know the Holy Ghost is not far away from them. We all know this is true. Any time we fast and pray and prepare ourselves we feel a greater influence of the Spirit, so we know he is never far from us.

2. Reading the scriptures daily

For me, this is the best way to feel the influence of the Holy Ghost. As I pray and read the scriptures or complete a lesson in the priesthood manual, I come to know that the Spirit is with me. I know that one cannot bear testimony that the scriptures are true unless he has the Holy Ghost as a companion. If you doubt this, have a nonmember or an inactive member read a passage in

---

3. Brigham Young, *Journal of Discourses,* 10:173.

the scriptures, and then ask them to bear testimony by the Spirit that it is true. They cannot do it. Therefore, when I am able to review the scriptures and feel in my heart and soul they are true, I know I am still on the strait and narrow path today.

3. Service in the kingdom of God

Sometimes as one serves for the right reasons, he will feel the influence of the Spirit. The right reason for service is to serve out of the love one feels for Heavenly Father and his son Jesus Christ.

Conclusion

1. One needs to draw unto Heavenly Father and feel his great love for him; one way to do this is by reading the scriptures and thus feeling one's spiritual worth.

2. As a person serves others and keeps the commandments, he does it with his mind and heart upon God and Jesus Christ. Then he will have good feelings about himself through the Holy Ghost. These good feelings will come even if his service is rejected by others.

3. If the person on the strait and narrow path seeks As, ten baptisms, material possessions, or honors from the community, he will do so for Heavenly Father and Jesus Christ. He will not do these things to prove his worth. It is vital that we all learn that feelings of true self-worth come only through the Holy Ghost; we can feel good about ourselves only as we open our hearts unto heaven. (Ephesians 6:5-8.)

4. As past sins come to the remembrance of the person on the path, he will choose to run through his mind and heart how Heavenly Father loves him and has forgiven him, as evidenced by feeling the Holy Ghost. He will no longer run past mistakes through his mind, discouraging and depressing him. Rather, he will concentrate on how to feel Heavenly Father's love and seek to grow spiritually.

As he does the above, he will know deep within his soul that he is forgiven of his sins. He will know he is clean and is a worthy candidate for the Celestial Kingdom. What peace this gospel understanding and application will bring unto him this day.

Section VI

SERVING OTHERS WITH THE LOVE OF GOD

All of us create barriers between ourselves and our Father in Heaven. These barriers separate us from God and thereby decrease our capacity to feel his love. Below are listed some of these barriers, along with the chapters that explains how the reader might remove each one. Review each barrier and check to see if any are still creating a problem for you.

Barriers that I use to separate myself from HIS LOVE

OK	Not OK	BARRIER	CHAPTER
☐	☐	Blaming self/others	11
☐	☐	Fears – worries – doubts	12
☐	☐	Believing that I am not good enough	7
☐	☐	Not seeking for HIS love	4
☐	☐	Feeling I have to be perfect to make it	10
☐	☐	Trying to prove my worth	1
☐	☐	Performance as main source for self-worth	7
☐	☐	Approval from others – main source for self-worth	7
☐	☐	Setting expectations above the mark	12
☐	☐	Not valuing myself as God does	7
☐	☐	Using guilt to punish myself	11
☐	☐	Using self-condemnation	11
☐	☐	Expecting no consequences from sin	12

Moroni, in chapter 7, reviewed several gospel areas that each individual must develop in order to expand his capacity to feel the pure love of Christ:

Verses:

40-41   One must have hope that he can gain eternal life. (This was developed in Section I.)

42   He must develop faith in the Savior.

43-44   He must be meek and lowly of heart. (This will be discussed in this section.)

44   He must be able to testify that Jesus is the Christ by the power of the Holy Ghost. (Reviewed in Section III.)

45-48   These verses define charity and how to be filled with it. (Reviewed in Section II and Section VI.)

What does it mean to be dependent upon God in all things? How can one exercise faith to the point of knowing God's mind and how God feels about him, even when he feels busy and everything is crushing in on him? How can he love and serve others when others do not appreciate the effort and even reject the person who gave it?

This section will try to answer these questions. It will provide the method whereby we can increase our capacity to feel the love of God and to feel love for all men, to be filled with the pure love of Christ, to better serve our fellowman, and to forgive all who trespass against us.

Chapter 13

Faith in Jesus Christ

FAITH, AS THE FIRST principle of the gospel, must be a part of our lives if we wish to eventually be exalted.

What does it mean to have faith in Jesus Christ?

Christ is the way: (John 14:6.) The person who believes in Christ and his way will be anxiously engaged in that way. He knows that following the Lord will bring him back into the presence of God. As he repents of his sins, he believes that Christ's way will cleanse him of his sins. He will treat himself with respect, as Christ would. He will seek the guidance of the Spirit. It will be natural for him to pray several times a day, as Christ surely did, as he seeks spiritual direction.

Christ is the truth: Truth frees one from spiritual darkness. It brings him into the light where peace, freedom, joy, and the power that enables one to endure to the end are found. To develop faith in Christ, he will seek the truth in the scriptures through the power of the Holy Ghost. His perceptions of the gospel will be correct and, therefore, the application of the gospel will bring joy. He will remember that truth comes of the Father, and that the opinions of others must be studied and verified before they can be accepted as truth.

Christ is the life: The person with faith believes that Christ gave life to all things, including himself. The power to live and breathe is centered in the light of Christ, which proceedeth forth from the presence of God. (D&C 88:7-13.) When he sees life in the flowers, trees, animals, sky, etc., he will recognize the source of that life. He will feel God's love for all mankind as he interacts with others, for in others he will recognize the light of Christ. He will also realize that gaining *eternal* life is achieved only through the grace of Christ, after he has done all he can do.

What has Christ done for me?

Our Condition Without Him

1. Sinful, unclean, not forgiven
2. Cut off from heaven
3. Never to return
4. No revelation
5. Never know our real identity
6. Not able to feel God's love
7. No resurrection, no hope in the grave
8. Walk in darkness, no light
9. No hope, no joy, no purpose
10. No eternal families
11. Devil and compulsion
12. No progression
13. Must atone for our own sins
14. Law of jungle
15. Hate and fear
16. No church or prophets

What Has The Savior Done For Me?

1. Overcame the grave and death
2. Paid for and suffered for repented sins
3. Our advocate with the Father
4. Organized Church, prophets
5. Gave us truth and knowledge
6. Taught us how to pray
7. What did he suffer for my sake?
   a. He bled from every pore (D&C 19:15-20.)
   b. He gave his life for my sake, his time, his very being. He was spat upon, laughed at, ridiculed, rejected, and killed for me.
   c. He fasted 40 days and nights, suffered, was tempted, and won for my sake.
8. Why did he do all this? Because of his love for Heavenly Father and me.

What Does He Ask For In Return?	What Will Interfere With This Relationship?
1. Repent — forsake and confess (D&C 58:42-43.)	1. Condemning myself
2. Bring forth fruit meet for repentance (Alma 12:15.)	2. Not recognizing or feeling my true identity
3. Help him save others (Moses 1:39.)	3. Not repenting (repentance is the pathway to feeling his love)
4. Be willing to suffer for him	4. Clinging to fears
5. Sacrifice for him	5. Not seeking truth and knowledge in scriptures
6. Love for him	6. Having doubts
7. Be like him	7. Having worldly performance, worldly view of self-worth
8. Forgive self and others	8. Underestimating Christ and His love
	9. Failing to ask
	10. Keeping my mind on myself. (Not loving self with unconditional love.)

As one studies the above, it becomes evident that Christ is the way, the truth, and the life. If we wish to achieve the goal of going back into the presence of God the Eternal Father, we can achieve it only through Christ.

What is Faith?

Joseph Smith taught:

Faith is the assurance of things hoped for, the evidence of things not seen. From this we learn that faith is the assurance which men have of the existence of things which they have not seen.... Faith ... is the moving cause of all action. [1]

The prophet went on to explain how faith operates. He said faith is built upon a hope for something that is unseen and is true; then one's faith stimulates action and exertion until the goal is attained. It takes faith to plant a garden, or go to work (because one needs faith to believe that he will be paid in two weeks), or to

---

1. *Lectures on Faith*, pp. 7, 8.

become educated. Joseph asks us the question, "Is there anything that you would have done, either physical or mental, if you had not previously believed?"

So what is faith? It is a *process* in which one hopes for something in the future, then believes he will obtain it, then by physical action he does obtain it. Belief alone is not enough: someone who only believes in something will not take the necessary action.

Jospeh Smith further said, "As faith is the moving cause of all action in temporal concerns, so it is in spiritual; for the Savior has said, ... He that *believeth* and is baptized shall be saved."

If a person has hope that he will be lifted up when the Savior comes, and if he progressively works on keeping the commandments, he is exercising faith in spiritual concerns. If a person believes he has great spiritual worth and treats himself and others in a special way because of this belief, he will receive "evidence of things not seen"! This is an exercise in spiritual matters, not temporal.

Faith is centered in whom?

Joseph Smith answered this question:

> We here observe that God is the only supreme governor and independent being in whom all fullness and perfection dwell: who is omnipotent, omnipresent, and omniscient; without beginning of days or end of life; and that he is the Father of lights; in him the principle of faith dwells independently, and he is the object in whom the faith of all other rational and accountable beings center for life and salvation. [2]

Joseph Smith taught that three things are necessary in order for one to exercise faith in God unto life and salvation. [3]

First, the idea that he actually exists.

---

2. Ibid., p. 13.
3. Ibid., p. 33.

Second, a *correct* idea of his character, perfections, and attributes.

For example, do we know that God is merciful and gracious, slow to anger, and never gives up on us?

> Is it not also necessary to have the idea that God is merciful and gracious, long-suffering and full of goodness? It is. Why is it necessary? Because of the weakness and imperfections of human nature, and the great frailties of man; for such is the weakness of man, and such his frailties, that he is liable to sin continually, and if God were not long-suffering and full of compassion, gracious and merciful, and of a forgiving disposition, man would be cut off from before him, in consequence of which he would be in continual doubt and could not exercise faith; *for where doubt is, there faith has no power;* but by man's believing that God is full of compassion and forgiveness, long-suffering and slow to anger, he can exercise faith in him and overcome doubt, so as to be exceedingly strong. [4]

Do we know that God is no respecter of persons and that he is love? In other words, he loves each of us with unconditional love. To know this is to keep alive and active one's hope of being raised unto eternal life. It is a truth that the more we know about the attributes of God, the greater our hope and, therefore, the greater our faith in him.

Third, an actual knowledge that the course of life which he is pursuing is according to the will of God, is essentially necessary to enable him to have the confidence in God without which no person can obtain eternal life.

Do you *believe* that you are in the strait and narrow path that leads unto life? Do you have *hope* that you will be raised up at the last day to meet the Savior? Do you have *faith* that your acts are preparing you for a celestial glory?

---

4. Ibid., pp. 38–39.

How to Obtain Faith Needed for Exaltation

Joseph Smith outlined the following important points:

> Let us here observe, that a religion that does not require *the sacrifice of all things temporally* never has the power sufficient to produce the faith necessary unto life and salvation; for, from the first existence of man, the faith necessary unto the enjoyment of life and salvation *never could be obtained without the sacrifice of all earthly things.* It is through the medium of the sacrifice of all earthly things that men do actually know that they are doing the things that are well pleasing in the sight of God. When a man has offered in sacrifice all that he has for the truth's sake, not even withholding his life, and believing before God that he has been called to make this sacrifice *because he seeks to do his will,* he does know, most assuredly, that God does and will accept his sacrifice and offering, and that he has not, nor will not seek his face in vain. Under these circumstances, then, he can obtain the faith necessary for him to lay hold on eternal life. [5]

What Happens When We Fail to Sacrifice?

But those who have not made this sacrifice to God do not know that the course which they pursue is well pleasing in his sight, for whatever may be their belief or their opinion, it is a matter of *doubt and uncertainty in their mind;* and *where doubt* and uncertainty are there faith is not, nor can it be. For doubt and faith do not exist in the same person at the same time; so that person whose mind is under doubt and fear cannot have unshaken confidence; and where unshaken confidence is not there faith is weak; and where faith is weak the person will not be able to contend against all the opposition, tribulations, and afflictions which they will have to encounter in order to be heirs of God, and joint heirs with Christ Jesus; *and they will grow weary in their minds, and the adversary will have* power over them and destroy them. [6]

---

5. Ibid., p. 58.

6. Ibid., pp. 59-60.

The Power of Unbelief

Unbelief brings spiritual darkness. (D&C 84:56.) It casts out light and cuts off the influence of the Spirit of the Lord. (Alma 32:28.) The unbelieving and fearful shall have their part in the lake which burneth. (Revelation 21:8.) Spiritual and temporal blessings cannot come to those who choose unbelief. For a person to not believe in himself brings sad consequences; it cuts off the power "to do." One then must rely on others for his support, which may include financial, emotional, and physical support. This dependency on others is a substitute for dependency on heaven.

Faith Takes Mental Exertion

We ask, then, what are we to understand by a man's working by faith? We answer—we understand that when a *man works by faith he works by mental exertion instead of physical force.* It is by words, instead of exerting his physical powers, with which every being works when he works by faith. God said, "Let there be light, and there was light." Joshua spake and the great lights which God had created stood still. Elijah commanded, and the heavens were stayed for the space of three years and six months, so that it did not rain: he again commanded and the heavens gave forth rain. All this was done by faith. And the Savior says, "If you have faith as a grain of a mustard seed, say to this mountain, 'Remove,' and it will remove; or say to that sycamore tree, 'Be ye plucked up, and planted in the midst of the sea;' and it shall obey you." Faith, then, *works by words; and with these its mightiest works have been, and will be, performed.* [7]

Joseph Smith tells us that angels move from place to place by the power of faith. The difference between one who is saved and one who is not is the degree of their faith. He suggests that as men begin *to live by faith* one can obtain heavenly visions, or the ministering of angels, or revelation. [8]

---

7. *Lectures on Faith,* p. 61.

8. Ibid., pp. 62, 63, 67.

We need to keep in mind that in the *physical world it takes labor to succeed*. Heavenly Father commanded, "By the sweat of thy face shalt thou eat bread, until thou shalt return unto the ground." (Moses 4:25.) But we also need to exercise faith to succeed in the physical world, as well as to grow spiritually.

Practice Exercising Your Faith

Yea, and how is it that ye have forgotten that the Lord is able to do all things according to his will, for the children of men, if it so be that they exercise faith in him? (1 Nephi 7:12.)

One day I was sitting in the temple and not feeling too well. I was tired physically and noticed that I wasn't really enjoying the temple session. In my mind I started playing a game. If God was here, I thought, I would feel spiritually alive. I would be at peace, receiving revelation and being moved to tears of joy and happiness.

Then the above scripture came to my mind, and I realized that I was projecting my sick feeling into my environment — and it is hard to feel a positive emotion and a negative emotion at the same time. That is, when I feel sick it is difficult to experience positive spiritual feelings. Next, I could see that I needed to exercise faith so I could maintain the thought that I knew Heavenly Father loved me and was pleased that I was serving him and others by being in the temple that day. As I maintained these thoughts, I felt great satisfaction come over me. I realized that my feeling of sickness could not separate me from the knowledge I had of how God felt at that hour.

That day I understood that when I exercised faith in Heavenly Father and his Son, no matter how I was feeling or what was happening in my environment, I could never be separated from that which I believed to be true. In the past I let my negative thoughts and feelings undermine the truth, and then I would be separated from that which I knew to be right. I would experience what it means to become a lone man in a dreary world.

Even though I still had sick feelings for the rest of the temple session, I was at peace — I *knew how God felt* even though I couldn't feel it from him directly.

Each person can exercise his faith daily in many areas of life, and he will be able to eventually overcome the effects of the world even though he does not have a great spiritual feeling each moment. We do not have the Holy Ghost with us every moment, but with faith we can *maintain* important spiritual feelings and thoughts:

1. To be forgiven of my sins (Enos 1:8.)
2. To know that God always loves me
3. To know and feel my spiritual worth
4. To have the hope that I will be lifted up unto eternal life (Moroni 7:41.)
5. To feel that my teenagers will make it
6. To love and serve others
7. To perform well spiritually (commandments)
8. To be protected (Alma 57:26-27.)
9. To feel the promise of sanctification (Ether 4:7.)

In addition, with faith and the gift of the Holy Ghost, we can experience healings (D&C 42:48-52.), receive revelation (Jarom 1:4), and see miracles occur.

It takes great mental exertion to maintain the state of mind of faith, particularly when one doesn't have the support of the environment or when one's emotional state is low. But it *can* be done, as one focuses this power that comes from heaven onto the spiritual dimension and receives the sustaining power that is needed during a crisis.

Joseph Smith was told by the Lord that all the fiery darts of the wicked cannot penetrate the shield of faith. (D&C 27:17.)

Heavenly powers are available to help an individual achieve greatness as he learns to concentrate his mind on selected righteous acts. To love God with all of one's heart takes great concentration.

The power "to do" comes from the spiritual nature of man, because when the spirit leaves the body, life is gone out of the body. Each person has the light of Christ in him, which provides this power "to do." (John 1:9.)

What is the source of our power?
(Life to Light)[9]

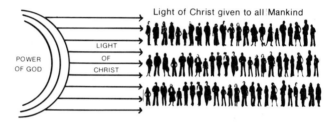

The light of Christ created the universe, including the sun and stars, and gives each person light. (D&C 88:7-10.) If this light of Christ is *concentrated* on a small surface, its power is multiplied.

For example, in Washington, D.C. there is a magnifying glass three feet in diameter. As the rays from ordinary sunlight touch this magnifying glass and these rays are focused below it, the heat becomes so great that it melts all instruments that try to measure its intensity. That is, ordinary sunlight (one aspect of the light of Christ), gathered together and concentrated in a small surface, becomes like a blow torch, melting steel like it was paper.

This same power is available to each person as he *concentrates his thoughts and feelings on a certain object until it is realized.* A temporal example would be a couple who desires to buy a home. They hold in their minds and hearts that desire for a home. They look at various homes, then save money for a home, read in magazines and newspapers about homes. In other words, they concentrate

---

9. *Melchizedek Priesthood Study Guide,* 1974-75, p. 80; D&C 88:5-13.

their power "to do" on this object until it is accomplished. They have *hope* that they will get a home. They *believe* that their dream home will be theirs, and they *act* on that belief and hope until it is realized.

A *spiritual* example would be when a child gets sick and a couple fasts and prays for his recovery. The power "to do" is concentrated on Heavenly Father and his power to heal. They hold *hope* in their minds and hearts for the recovery of this child; they *believe* in God's power to heal; and they *act* by fasting and prayer. This creates spiritual power in their minds and therefore the powers of heaven are available to them. This is why Joseph Smith said that "faith is the principle of power."[10]

Joseph Smith went on to demonstrate, by examples of the past, that there is great power in faith:

> Through faith we understand that the worlds were framed...it was the faith of Alma and Amulek which caused the walls of the prison to be rent...it was the faith of Nephi and Lehi which caused a change to be wrought upon the hearts of the Lamanites...faith subdued kingdoms, wrought righteousness, obtained promises, stopped the mouths of lions...the violence of fire...and that women received their dead raised to life again.[11]

The problems of the physical world were overcome through the spiritual dimension. Each sought power from heaven and received it.

Man has the power to abstain from sin in direct proportion to his faith in God. The greater the faith, the greater the power to do righteousness and overcome sin and temptations. Joseph Smith explained,

> [Jesus] is called the Son because of the flesh, and descended in suffering below that which man can suffer;

---

10. *Lectures on Faith*, p. 9.

11. Ibid., p. 9.

or in other words, suffered greater sufferings, and was exposed to more powerful contradictions than any man can be. But, notwithstanding all this, he kept the law of God, and remained without sin, showing thereby that *it is in the power of man to keep the law and remain also without sin.* [12]

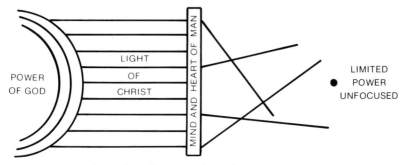

Latter-day Saint using the Light of Christ with no definite spiritual goals or commitments.

This person has limited power to do because the light is not concentrated but scattered. Some rays do not get through to his mind because he doubts his abilities, worth, or worries about his progress.

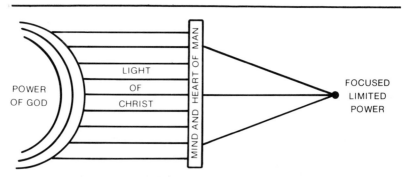

Latter-day Saint using the Light of Christ in concentrating on a negative goal.

This person has many doubts, worries, and fears that block out the light of Christ, and he has concentrated his power "to do" on a negative goal. He has lost his wife through a divorce and his mind and heart are centered on her and how much he needs her.

---

12. Ibid., p. 48.

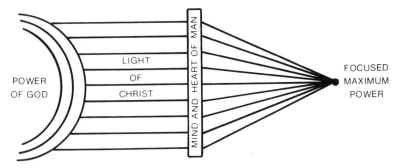

Latter-day Saint using the Light of Christ for spiritual and temporal success

This person has focused his life on eternal life and salvation. Most rays come through because faith and love cast out all fear and doubts. He recognizes his dependence upon Christ and seeks for spiritual growth. He can be successful in this life and the next.

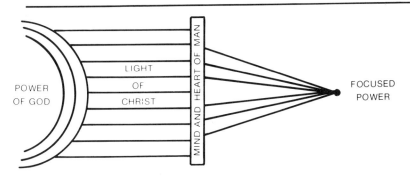

Natural Man using the Light of Christ for temporal success.

This person has focused his life on gaining power in this life. His energy is spent on gaining money and power over others. He is very successful in his efforts. He has learned to use his power "to do" for his selfish purposes. He believes in himself and fears little. He has no experience with spiritual realities.

How to Grow Spiritually

In the Book of Mormon, Alma reviewed in detail the steps one must take in order to grow spiritually by exercising his faith. Notice that Alma is discussing growth in the spiritual dimension

and not in the temporal. To get the most out of this section, read
the scripture noted, then the commentary below.

Alma 32:27   Desire to believe

Alma 28   Do not cast it out by unbelief and resist the Spirit
of the Lord.

A person must choose which emotion will be
dominant.

A person who desires to feel his spiritual worth
will value himself as God values him. He will study
the scriptures and the prophets to understand
who he is. He treats himself as a son of God, born
and reared in the courts of glory by heavenly
parents. He prays, expresses his love to God, and
feels God's love for him by the power of the Holy
Ghost.

Alma 28   The evidence for knowing that feeling of spiritual
worth *is a good seed.*

1. Swells within his breast (he feels good
inside, excited).

2. Enlightens one's understanding (he comes
to understand that his worth in the eyes of God is
not based on his performance).

3. Begins to be delicious to him (because of
the joy of feeling accepted, he desires to do more
to draw closer unto Heavenly Father).

Alma 29–30   He will come to recognize that the seed is good and
can feel his faith increase.

Alma 31–32   Can he be sure it is a good seed? Yes, if it grows—
and it did.

Alma 34   Would he now have perfect knowledge? Yes, in
that he knows it is a good seed. He also knows that
he is a son of God and has great worth.

Alma 37–38   Now he wants the seed to become a tree and

produce fruit. What must he do for the seed to take root in his mind and heart, and become a part of him?

He must *exercise his faith* by giving his spiritual worth much thought, by recalling who he is and how much God loves him. He will do this several times a day. He will develop deep emotions about these thoughts.

He knows if he gives his spiritual worth no thought, he will forget all about it and will have to look to others, or his possessions, or his performance in order to feel his worth.

Alma 40   He will nourish his spiritual worth with faith, which means he will envision the results in his life as he becomes dependent upon God, and not the world, for his worth. He will have an increased ability to give love, increased guidance from the Holy Ghost, increased ability to endure rejection, and increased sense of qualifying for celestial glory.

Alma 41   The belief in his spiritual value will take root and become an integral part of his personality and be influential in directing one's life. This is accomplished by:

    1. Continuing to nourish the thought as it begins to grow; repeating the thought and feeling it.

    2. Exercising faith; seeing the fruit of the tree with great patience and diligence.

At times he will forget who he is, or not see the worth of another person. But he will seek to get back on track by feeding his mind and heart with thoughts of who he is and of the worth of all God's children. He will not choose to condemn himself because he has slipped. Diligence means that he will never give up, while patience provides the atmosphere for him to forgive himself.

Alma 42-43 Then one day someone will reject him and put him down. He will find himself seeking God's help to understand the accuser and showing forth love and understanding. Then both he and the other person are edified. He feels deeply about who he is and treats himself and others with respect and awe.

Alma 32 teaches the following about faith:
1. What is faith?
2. How to use faith to grow spiritually.
3. How to plant spiritual thoughts and ideas.
4. How to know if the thought or idea is good.
5. How to use the principle of "exercising one's faith."
6. The importance of emotions in spiritual growth.
7. The importance of seeing and feeling the end result.
8. The importance of patience with self in the growth process.
9. The importance of diligence in one's spiritual effort.

What does it mean to have faith in the Savior?

It means that a person has confidence in what he has chosen to do, for he desires to follow the Master. It means that he has removed doubts that would interfere with this confidence. He chooses to feel how God loves him, even though he is separated from God. He takes responsibility for his relationship with his Father in Heaven, and responsibility to feel his great personal spiritual worth. He senses his weaknesses and his unworthiness at times, but chooses to seek spiritual growth rather than self-condemnation. He expands his knowledge by study and by faith, so he can see more clearly and draw closer to God and Christ. He will not weaken his faith by recalling his past sins or playing games with Satan. He has faith that he will qualify for celestial inheritance, and he seeks confirmation of that daily. He recognizes that as his faith grows, his capacity to love expands, and he senses this growth as he relates to others. At the same time his endurance for rejection is greater, and he finds greater joy in giving.

Chapter 14

Dependence Upon God In All Things

BEING HUMBLE, BEING MEEK, recognizing our dependence on God—these are essential attitudes for the person who seeks to walk the strait and narrow path which leads to life eternal.

What does it mean to be meek and lowly of heart?

Meekness means to not put oneself above another. It means to sense the greatness in others, to feel the value that God places on them as persons of worth. It is to sense the uniqueness of others, to be willing to listen with love and respect. To be meek is not to be timid. The meek person has confidence in himself and seeks to do that which is righteous. He is a doer and not a hearer only. He has gained self-confidence and love for others because of his relationship with God. He feels the love God has for him and senses the value God has placed upon him. It therefore is easy for him to love his neighbor as himself, for his love for both neighbor and himself comes from God's dimension. He desires to love as God loves, be kind as God is kind, be just as God is just, be merciful as God is merciful, and so forth. He values himself and others as God does. He seeks to love others with God's love.

Mormon sought to love the wicked Nephites as God would.

> *Behold, I had led them, notwithstanding their wickedness I had led them many times to battle, and had loved them,* **according to the love of God which was in me,** *with all my heart.* (Mormon 3:12.)

A meek person is strong because of his faith in God, but he is a person others enjoy being around because he is a gentle, loving, and caring person. One feels uplifted in a meek person's presence and senses the presence of the Spirit. Why does a person feel uplifted? Because the meek person doesn't look down upon him but treats him as an equal. It is a good feeling to experience.

To be lowly of heart is for a person to recognize his dependence upon God in all things. A meek person like Moses is a doer, a leader, a person of great confidence — but he also was lowly of heart. He sought to do the will of his Father in Heaven. The Savior was gentle and meek. He drove the moneychangers out of the temple; he spoke out to let the Sadducees and Pharisees know of their spiritual problems; but he said of himself, "I am meek and lowly in heart." (Matthew 11:29.) The Savior submitted his will unto the will of the Father in all things.

Dependence upon the Father, Son, and Holy Ghost

In order for man to overcome the world he must recognize his dependence upon God the Father and his Son Jesus Christ, as well as the Holy Ghost, through whom he feels God's power and influence.

In the *Melchizedek Priesthood Study Guide* (1974–75) is recorded the following:

> Do you feel that you depend upon the Savior for your spiritual and temporal well-being? Or do you suppose that your own genius and strength are sufficient to guarantee you day-to-day success?

It is possible to succeed beyond one's natural ability as he recognizes his dependence upon Christ. [1]

In order for a person to be successful in this life he must consider four areas of life: personal, family, vocation, and kingdom responsibilities. To succeed in all four areas takes great effort and concentration. The world teaches that if one is successful in his vocation, attaining high position or creating great wealth, he will be respected by his peers — even if he loses his family and is not active in the spiritual dimension. Not so with celestial achievement. One needs to be successful in all four areas of life. The saying goes, "One can *live* without God, but he cannot *succeed* without Him."

To succeed in all four areas requires a dependence upon God and Jesus Christ. One's natural abilities are never sufficient. Sometimes a heart needs to be touched, a door opened, a loved one healed. Sometimes we need increased strength to endure, or increased light and knowledge in order to adjust. All such needed assistance comes through the spiritual dimension.

Let us review several scriptures that suggest that our success in this life depends upon our relationship with the Godhead. They are the source of our spiritual strength.

> *Yea, I know that I am nothing; as to my strength I am weak; therefore I will not boast of myself, but I will boast of my God, for in his strength I can do all things.* (Alma 26:12)

> *I am the vine, ye are the branches: He that abideth in me, and I in him, the same bringeth forth much fruit: for without me ye can do nothing.* (John 15:5)

> *The Lord is my strength ... he is my salvation.* (Exodus 15:2)

> *I can do all things through Christ which strengtheneth me.* (Philippians 4:13)

> *I know, in the strength of the Lord thou canst do all things.* (Alma 20:4)

---

1. *Melchizedek Priesthood Study Guide*, 1974–75, pp. 82, 87.

And the light which shineth, which giveth you light, is through him who enlighteneth your eyes, which is the same light that quickeneth your understanding . . . the light which is in all things, which giveth life to all things, which is the law by which all things are governed, even the power of God. (D&C 88:11–13)

With Christ's Help I Can Carry My Cross

And he that taketh not his cross, and followeth after me,
is not worthy of me." (Matthew 10:38.)

What was this cross? He carried the burden of all our sins and met the demands of justice for each person who repents. What are some of the crosses we have to bear? Being divorced, not being married, financial problems, health problems, teenagers struggling, or parents who need one's help? Now is it possible to bear these crosses, while one is growing spiritually? "Those who have endured the crosses of the world . . . they shall inherit the Kingdom of God." (2 Nephi 9:18.)

In Lehi's dream he saw a spacious building filled with people who make fun of those who take upon them the cross of the Savior. Those who made it and endured were those *who recognized their dependence upon Christ.* Those who didn't make it were those *who put their dependence on others.* The rejection by others was too great for them to stay in the strait and narrow path.

Philosophy of Self-Sufficiency

What is the opposite of this dependence upon Christ? The philosophy of self-sufficiency. Stephen L. Richards explained the differences between the two philosophies:

Why is it so difficult to accept things of faith? I think I can suggest an answer. It is because we are so conceited. Men of the world are in the world only because they adopt the philosophy of the world, which is the philosophy of self-sufficiency. It is not a humble philosophy—it is highly egotistical. It makes men themselves the arbiters of all things. They look to no higher source than themselves for the solution to all questions.

Such a philosophy is diametrically opposed to the philosophy of Christ, which is that of faith. When men adopt his philosophy they are humble — they acknowledge an intelligence far superior to their own and they seek guidance and wisdom from that source. When they adopt the philosophy of faith, they come out of the world, for the world, as a term in theology, is not a place but a condition of a state of mind and feeling. It requires courage to come out of the world and adopt the philosophy of faith. Sometimes it subjects one to ridicule and to contempt of friends, which are harder for most men to endure than physical pain; but because a thing is hard to do or hard to believe is no assurance that it is not right.

I am one, however, who believes that it is not so hard for most people to have faith and accept spiritual realities if they will but let their minds and their native inclinations pursue their natural bent. I think that altogether too often we permit thinking complexes and sophisticated reasoning to warp our intuitive judgment and entrammel the spontaneous feeling and emotions of our soul. So, when I prescribe that acceptance of Christ as a condition of orthodoxy, I mean an acceptance without reservation — a whole-souled, intelligent, joyous acceptance of him that proclaims him Lord, Savior, Redeemer and Mediator with the Father and lays claim on his mercy, his grace and his love for all the finer things we know in life — what hope, what peace and satisfaction such a full acceptance of the Christ brings to the heart of man, only those who have received a testimony of Jesus will ever know![2]

Law of Consecration, a Celestial Law

When we recognize our dependence on God, we see that our lives, our possessions, and the earth itself belong to God. We then

---

2. Stephen L. Richards, *Conference Report,* April 1935, pp. 30-31.

understand that consecration is one of the highest — and most necessary—expressions of love.

> Consecration is the giving of one's own time, talents, and means to care for those in need — whether spiritually or temporally — and in building the Lord's kingdom . . . we consecrate when we give of ourselves. [3]

The United Order is one vehicle to carry out the law of consecration. Enoch and his city lived the United Order and they therefore were lifted up. God and Jesus Christ live a consecrated life. For a person to enjoy the celestial kingdom he must consecrate his time, talents, property, and his very life to God. This becomes easy as he learns to love God with all his heart, might, mind, and strength, and his neighbor as himself.

Concerning consecrating all that one has to build up the kingdom, someone has said that God has asked only for a promissory note from his children. Someday he will call that note, at which time each person will be able to fulfill his commitment.

What can one do today to prepare for that day of full commitment?

First, a person must develop the capacity to feel God's love for himself and his neighbor. He must remove the barriers that limit this capacity. He must feel after Heavenly Father daily, expressing love to him and desiring to serve him, thereby drawing closer unto him.

Second, he must consecrate all that he has to Heavenly Father and Jesus Christ NOW. Joseph Smith said,

> When we consecrate our property to the Lord it is to administer to the wants of the poor and needy, for this is the law of God.... Now for a man to consecrate his

---

3. Spencer W. Kimball, *The Teachings of Spencer W. Kimball,* (Salt Lake City, Utah: Bookcraft, 1982,) p. 366.

property, wife and children, to the Lord, is nothing more nor less than to feed the hungry, clothe the naked, visit the widow and the fatherless, the sick and afflicted, and do all he can do to administer to their relief in their afflictions, and for him and his home to serve the Lord."[4]

Therefore, all that one possesses belongs to Heavenly Father — his cars, house, time, talents, family, and all else. He now has a stewardship responsibility over these various possessions and family members. He is accountable for what he does with his physical body, his spiritual development, his talents, his bills, his assets. He no longer sees his possessions as an extension of himself, but as assets owned by God, which he is asked to administer.

When the neighbor asks to use the lawnmower, then, it's okay because the mower belongs to God anyway. If the neighbor brings it back damaged, the consecrated person will not choose to develop bad feelings toward the neighbor, but only asks the neighbor to repair it. If the neighbor refuses, so be it. Even if our friend has to pay money to repair the mower, he does it unto God and keeps bad feelings from lingering in his heart. If the neighbor asks to borrow the lawnmower again, and our friend feels that Heavenly Father approves, then he will gladly help his neighbor. And since our friend represents Heavenly Father in this item, he will feel good about explaining to his neighbor the need to return the equipment in workable order.

Each person has a stewardship over his assets or income to provide for his family and his retirement, and to build the kingdom. If he invests in a project that loses money, he will not choose to dislike the promoter or sue the salesman. Rather, he will forgive them, since Heavenly Father will forgive our friend for investing in something that lost the money. Since the money that was lost belongs to Heavenly Father, those who lost it will have to be accountable to God.

---

4. *Teachings of the Prophet Joseph Smith,* p. 127.

At times one may feel impressed to sue someone so as to keep them from harming others. The purpose of the suit is to teach and prevent, not to get even.

Saints have learned to love their enemies and those who harm them. They also have learned to stand up for God and what is *His.* They are good stewards, because they treat their neighbors as themselves and administer Heavenly Father's goods in righteousness. They believe that all they possess belongs to God.

Third, one seeks for ways to administer to the poor, sick, and afflicted. Welfare assignments are sought after, for this is Heavenly Father's way of teaching one to sacrifice for others. It is His way to provide for the poor. He seeks to give unto those who are dead physically through temple work and genealogy, for he sees his time as the Lord's. Whether his time is used to work, teach a Sunday School class, or do home teaching, go to the temple, serve on a mission, go golfing, or do physical exercise, it is all committed unto Heavenly Father.

As one does the above, it will provide the necessary growth to live the full law of consecration when the Lord calls his promissory note, for he will have developed the right attitude toward his possessions, his neighbors, his self, and his time. The United Order can provide the atmosphere for one to love God and his neighbor correctly. In the meantime, each of us can make progress toward the goal of loving God with all our hearts, might, minds, and strength. And when the time arrives to live the United Order, and our preparation is over, we are ready to do that which we have prayed for and dreamed of, that is, having all things equal, with the rich made low and the poor exalted. We will have all things in common. We will be prepared in every way to enter the celestial kingdom.

In conclusion, if a person wishes to be dependent upon God in all things, he will seek spiritual enlightenment in all facets of his life. In order not to let the cares of this world interfere with his relationship with Heavenly Father, he will see his worldly goods as gifts from heaven, and he will acknowledge that he is administering these goods for heaven. If something is misused by his neighbor, so be it — it belongs to God anyway. He can be firm with his neighbor, but only for the purpose of taking better care of God's property. He will seek to feed and clothe the poor, the sick, and the afflicted, which could include his own family at times. His love for God increases, because he can see and feel the joys that come from doing all things unto God. He has increased his capacity to receive the pure love of Christ from Heavenly Father, because he has fulfilled the requirement to be meek and lowly of heart. He truly is on the strait and narrow path to eternal life.

Chapter 15

Serving Others With The Pure Love of Christ

As you have read through this book, we have traveled on a journey together. As we walked in the strait and narrow path each day, seeking and receiving guidance through the power of the Holy Ghost, we have been able to develop stronger spiritual feelings. These feelings have been sufficient to keep us under the influence of the Spirit, even when the pressures of this temporal world have increased from time to time. When we became upset over money or family problems, it became very clear that the Holy Ghost had withdrawn from us. Therefore, we sought Heavenly Father in our difficulty and received the guidance of the Holy Ghost again. It has gradually become easier to recognize when the Spirit withdraws, and we have been able to diminish the effects of temporal pressures by seeking the solutions through the spiritual dimension.

After applying the principles in this book, we are now experiencing a never-ending supply of feelings of love for God, ourselves, and others. We have learned to place our minds upon

Heavenly Father and seek to feel, value, and love as he does. Somedays we feel sick, depressed, or frustrated. It is impossible to experience feelings of love when we feel these negative emotions. But as we place our minds upon Heavenly Father and value ourselves and others as he values us, it is easy to feel love, even though we may not be feeling very well at the time.

We have learned that it is possible to feel pure feelings of love for all people, regardless of their actions, and we know that the source of these emotions is Heavenly Father. The more we have drawn on this source the easier it has been to maintain dominating feelings of love for God as we walk through the battlefield of life. We now recognize that we have access to an endless reservoir of love. This reservoir of love, or charity, represents the feelings we have for God, ourselves, and others. Its source is from above, and we have access to it as we seek to open our minds and hearts unto Heavenly Father and to feel as he feels. We receive this great gift as we qualify for it and desire to love ourselves and others with God's love.

We have learned that it is important to correctly apply the gospel in our lives if we wish to maintain access to this reservoir. We have learned that as we maintain access to God's reservoir it is easier to have our dominating emotions centered in the spiritual. To love God with all our hearts becomes easier, because we seek to love as he loves, which we are able to do as we place our minds upon him. We now are seeking to grow spiritually by making the following gospel principles and goals realities in our lives:

1. We now have a perfect brightness of hope that we will be raised unto eternal life; all doubts are removed.
2. We understand that our personal worth is not based upon performance—but we know feeling God's love is based upon spiritual performance.
3. We seek to interact with the spiritual dimension and receive revelation.

4. We now overcome the problems of the world through the spiritual dimension.
5. We know how to keep all the commandments and enjoy them.
6. We know that guilt feelings are good, because they help us draw closer to Heavenly Father.
7. We understand that the demands of justice are designed to help us gain eternal life.
8. We know that a good parent is one who loves and teaches and is not judged according to what the child chooses to do.
9. We no longer condemn ourselves when making mistakes.
10. We understand that expressing our feelings verbally is an act of love.
11. We know we are forgiven of all our sins, even though we still are overcoming the effects of walking in spiritual darkness.
12. When past sins come into our minds, we recognize our mistakes but then seek to feel the Spirit and serve God.
13. We value ourselves as God values us.
14. We value others as God values them.
15. We feel God's love for us and others.
16. The more we feel God's love, the more we want to do good and serve him by serving others.
17. We acknowledge that all our possessions belong to Heavenly Father.
18. We understand that when we feel each day how much God loves us, we are exercising our faith.
19. We recognize that we have a responsibility to feel God's love for ourselves and others.
20. We know that the best way to serve our fellowman is with the pure love of Christ that we feel within our souls. That pure love comes as we open our hearts unto Heavenly Father.

The more we apply these principles, the greater we expand our capacity to love God and draw upon his reservoir of love. The more we draw upon this reservoir, the more we can lengthen our stride and endure the adversities of this life. Adversities tend to draw us away from God and, therefore, from this reservoir of love. Problems tend to draw emotional energy from us, and the greater the problems (both in intensity and number), the greater the drain.

The only way to gain access to the reservoir again is to turn our minds from the problems and to seek solutions with God's help. As our minds and energy concentrate on the solutions to the problems, the light of Christ can enlighten our minds, which produces hope and thereby increases our energy. It takes time to turn our minds to solutions, for if the emotions created by the problems are greater than the emotions of hope for the solution, the problems will remain in center stage. It takes time and effort to create dominating emotions of hope.

It is clear that each of us can affect our spiritual growth and draw closer unto Heavenly Father. Blessed is he who feels his spiritual worth and the worth of others. Blessed is he who knows of the deep love God has for him. Blessed is he who can see clearly how to overcome this world and enjoy it to its fullest.

The demands of justice are exact, but as one feels the love of God in his heart, he will do all that is necessary to benefit from Christ's sacrifice, which meets the demands of justice for the repentant. When a person cannot feel the love that God has for him, the burdens become too great to endure—he feels alone; the joys of this life are gone; he knows what is true but cannot find the ways to enjoy it.

But as we serve God with all our heart, might, mind, and strength and our neighbor as ourselves, we will receive the gifts of happiness, peace, and joy. Most of all, we will qualify to be raised up unto eternal life, which is my strongest desire.

ASSIGNMENT

Number one: When you do your home teaching or visiting teaching this month, first seek to feel the pure love of Christ, and then serve the families out of these feelings of love. Watch to see if you feel greater love and joy out of this kind of service.

Number two: Before going to church this Sunday, seek to be filled with this pure love of Christ, then commit to Heavenly Father that you are prepared to serve the poor, sick, and afflicted, at the next opportunity, by joining with others on the welfare farm. Do the assignment not out of necessity but out of the love you feel for God and his Son.

> *But this I say, He which soweth sparingly shall reap also sparingly; and he which soweth bountifully shall reap also bountifully.*
>
> *Every man according as he purposeth in his heart, so let him give; not grudgingly, or of necessity: for God loveth a cheerful giver.*
>
> *And God is able to make all grace abound toward you; that ye, always having all sufficiency in all things, may abound to every good work.* (2 Cor. 9:6-8.)

Number three: Plan ahead situations where you know you will be rejected or made to feel ill at ease. Prepare yourself spiritually and seek to maintain good feelings toward the individuals, even though they are rejecting you. Do good unto them, but do it for Heavenly Father and the Savior. Observe how you are able to control your emotions and the environment by being spiritually in control.

Number four: First prepare yourself spiritually for this assignment by feeling the love Heavenly Father has for you. Now run through your mind and heart your past mistakes, and concentrate on forgiving yourself by experiencing deep feelings of love. You will observe that you have a choice. You can either recall past sins, feel bad about the sins, and then transfer these feelings to yourself, or you can forgive yourself and fill the present moments with feelings of love that are stronger than the emotions created by recalling past sins. When you have developed the ability to love yourself with the kind of love God has, making these feelings dominant over all other feelings, you will be able to recall past mistakes and have no feelings of bitterness. ("No bitterness of past frictions can be held in memory if we forgive with all our hearts."[1])

Number five: Recall someone who has harmed you. Practice feeling God's love for them, even with their mistakes. Set a goal to develop stronger feelings of love for God — stronger than your negative feelings of hate or distrust or rejection. Develop these feelings by experiencing God's love for them, go forth with these feelings of pure love and do something good for them. Bless them. Do not seek for any return from them, for you are only in the service of your God. (Read Ephesians 6:5-8.)

---

1. Spencer W. Kimball, *Conference Report,* Sept. 1949, pp. 132-33.

APPENDIX A

Here is a listing of one hundred examples of laws, ordinances, or commandments which a group of Latter-day Saints recently listed as necessary for them to reach the Celestial Kingdom:

1. Charity
2. Faith in Savior
3. Repent
4. Baptism
5. Holy Ghost
6. Endure to End
7. Tithing
8. Exercise
9. Church
10. Community service
11. Serve country
12. Fasting
13. Fast offering
14. Budget, bldg. fund
15. Genealogy
16. Personal prayer
17. Home/Visit. Teaching
18. Temple work
19. Temple marriage
20. Sacrament Meeting
21. Priesthood/Relief S.
22. Sunday School
23. Family prayer
24. Word of Wisdom
25. Scripture study
26. Missionary work
27. Family Home Ev.
28. Sabbath day
29. No other gods
30. No graven images
31. Lords name in vain
32. Honor parents
33. Do not kill
34. No adultery
35. No false witness
36. No coveting
37. Plant garden
38. Journals
39. Ward choir
40. Year supply
41. Follow Prophet/leaders
42. Be of good cheer
43. No stealing
44. No fault finding
45. Provide for family
46. Be honest
47. Virtuous thoughts
48. Read good books
49. Administer to sick
50. Forgive others
51. World/current events
52. Teach children
53. Sleep
54. Magnify callings
55. Lengthen stride
56. Feed missionaries
57. Return/Borrow
58. Bear Testimony
59. No light mindedness
60. Develop talents
61. Become perfect
62. Law of Consecration
63. Law of Sacrifice
64. Recreation
65. Control own thoughts
66. Visit elderly
67. Personal & Fam. histories
68. Organize home

69. Be humble
70. Fellowship
71. Good example
72. Obey laws of land
73. Love God & all men
74. Shop wisely
75. Out of debt
76. Have children
77. Personal Prsthd. interview
78. Patriarchal blessing
79. Perfect hope
80. Cease to be idle
81. Golden rule
82. Avoid evil
83. Love self
84. Control appetites/passions
85. Sense of humor
86. Welfare projects
87. Husb./wife dates
88. Don't fight/quarrel
89. Peacemaker
90. Communicate
91. Paint house, fix yard
92. Defend truth
93. Be patient
94. Tolerance
95. Do it (doer)
96. Help Lamanites
97. Family councils
98. Do not swear
99. Social development
100. Be friendly

"Becoming Spiritually Centered and Overcoming The World"
on AUDIO CASSETTES

(see next page for content)

These audio cassettes (including a seminar manual)
are available for only $60.00. Order from your local
bookstore, or, you may mail your order to the address
below. (Please add $5.00 for shipping and handling)

You may mail your order and money to:

National Marketing, INC
P.O. Box 3305
Nampa, ID 83653
Phone: (208) 442-0040
Email: nmiut.8482@gmail.com
Website: www.nmiut.com

and then mail your check to
National Marketing, Inc.

"Becoming Spiritually Centered and Overcoming The World"
on AUDIO CASSETTES

These cassette tapes are a live recording of Brother Cox giving his eight week seminar teaching the participates on HOW to become spiritually centered. He first teaches them the steps necessary to change thought patterns. Next he reviews twelve thought patterns of the Savior so the participates can compare their thought patterns. Those thoughts that do not match the Saviors can now be changed, with spiritual results. The highlights of each tape is as follows:

ONE -The purpose of the Day
-Your Three worlds
-Process for change
-12 thought patterns of Christ

TWO -Hope to be raised unto eternal Life
-Plan of Salvation & feeling the Spirit
-How to Qualify for the Celestial Kingdom

THREE -Developing low feelings of self-worth
-Developing high feelings of Self-Worth

FOUR -The purpose of performance
-Charity - the pure love of Christ
-Using the day for spiritual growth

FIVE -Seeing all things spiritually
-the Law of Consecration

SIX -Using enticements for spiritual growth
-How to be thankful in your adversities

SEVEN -I am in charge of what I think, feel, and do
-Changing my expectations
-Disowning & the prices I pay

EIGHT -I am not responsible for what others do
-My stewardship responsibility

NINE -Turn back to God and live
-Worldly Sorrow - Godly Sorrow

TEN -Love God and Trust in Him
-Grace vs. Works

ELEVEN -The gift of forgiveness
-Judging for progression
-What to do now that the seminar is over

TWELVE -Planning your day for spiritual growth

Over 8,000 people have attended Brother Cox's seminars on Becoming Spiritually Centered and Overcoming the world. They have learned how to use the temporal world for spiritual growth. Many participants have developed high feelings of self-worth, along with seeing Heavenly Father's hand in the details of their daily life. They are using enticements for spiritual growth and they are experiencing the difference as they learn to become one with Christ, by seeing as He sees, feeling and thinking as He does, and doing as He would do in the same situation. These cassettes will take what you already know and show you how to apply it in all situations.